SO FAR, SO GOOD

(...but it was touch and go there for a while)

JODY MCBRAYER

LUCIDBOOKS

For Sonny

TABLE OF CONTENTS

FOREWORD

Here is a man who has a beautiful and unusual tenor voice. He is a number-one recording artist. He has a strong stage presence, is well-spoken, knows the Scriptures, has a beautiful wife and daughter, has traveled the world, lives in Nashville—all of his dreams have obviously come true.

Jody McBrayer's successes have been beyond his wildest expectations, but sadly, so have his hurts. This book will describe in great detail how the lows in Jody's life were even greater than his highs. And they almost cost him his voice and his life.

Jody was 17 when his dad introduced me to him after a TRUTH concert. Jody wanted to sing in the group, but I suggested he get two years of college first. During those two years, he roomed with two of my sons and in many ways became a son.

He was always listening to and had an ear for new music. One day on our tour bus, he handed me his headphones and said, "You've gotta hear this new singer. She's going to be huge!" It was Celine Dion!

After he left TRUTH, we stayed in touch. Some years I watched his many successes from afar. Some years we talked about his frustrations, his deep hurts, and the decisions he was considering. On other occasions we talked about life, his health, and old times. I know in the early years he missed his dad greatly, and that loss had a profound effect on many aspects of his life and career.

Jody's story is a reminder of God's promise to never leave us, even though there are times He is silent when we choose our own way. God's hand on Jody's journey is exciting, sometimes sad, yet a huge encouragement for the reader. I read a quote recently that reminded me of Jody's journey. "God is never without options, so we are never without hope."

For literally hundreds of nights, I listened as Jody sang his signature song with TRUTH—"We have come so far, and You have been so good." I have no doubt as you read about the path that God has led Jody down that you will absolutely agree that God has brought Jody so far, and through it all, He has been so good.

Emerson once wrote, "Greatness is he who reminds you of no other." Jody is truly unique and has achieved great things, but he strives to lead with a heart for Christ and to use what the enemy hoped would destroy him to help others. To me, that is greatness.

—Roger Breland
Special Assistant to the President of the University of Mobile
Director, Roger Breland Center for Performing Arts
Dean Emeritus, Voices of Mobile
Founder and Director of TRUTH

PROLOGUE:
THE STALEMATE

October 2014

I was restless. Nothing was making me comfortable or happy. I jumped up because I thought a walk on the beach might settle my nerves.

It was 3:00 a.m., so I had the night to myself. I walked to the top of one of the beach access points and looked out at the ocean. There was no moon, and the sky was crystal clear and full of stars. I could see the stars reflected on the surface of the water, and it looked so peaceful. The peace seemed to be calling me, so I walked down the steps and put my feet in the sand. I was surprised that the sand was still warm, especially for an October night.

I walked toward the shore until both feet were in the water. The waves were calm and lapped the sand in a way that was mesmerizing, almost hypnotic. I started walking so I could feel the water on my feet, and then . . . I just kept walking.

My family and I joke about it now because we're fans of Discovery Channel's Shark Week, and many attacks happen at night. I often shout at people on TV who decide to go for an evening swim in the ocean. "What about the sharks, people? Do you not know that night is prime feeding time?" But that night, the thought never occurred to me. My mind was very far from making any kind of logical decision.

I walked in until the water was above my waist, and it was so still. I wasn't getting pushed around by waves or the current. If I hadn't seen the sky wrapping around me in every direction, I would have sworn I was walking in a swimming pool. I looked up at the sky sparkling back down at me and said aloud, "You're not there. I've spent my entire life doing everything You wanted me to do, and granted, I've made some mistakes, but each time I always ran back to You because I knew You'd be there to help me. What happened? Where have You been? It's like You're just gone. I'm tired. I can't handle any of this anymore."

I looked out at the horizon and saw what looked like the glow of the coming sunrise. But it was still the middle of the night, and never mind that I was on the Florida Panhandle and not even facing east. I saw a glow on the horizon and thought, *That's where I'm going.* In the same way the water had lured me in with its peace, this glowing light was calling me to come to it.

I know now it was darkness—the enemy trying to make going deeper as appealing as possible—because a few more steps and I would have been in over my head. That warm water, the soft breeze, the sky so full of stars—everything was perfect. Now I see it was more like a perfect storm to convince me to follow what I thought would finally bring some peace to my weariness.

I've heard people describe death by drowning before. They say your lungs fill up with water, you struggle for about 30 seconds, and then the most peaceful feeling overtakes you. I thought, *If I can just make it through 30 seconds, I'll be with my dad when it's over. I'll be home.*

I missed my dad desperately. Everything was always okay when I was with him. Even when life wasn't okay, he had a unique way of making me feel in my bones that it was going to be okay. Nothing seemed okay anymore. Even what others perceived as okay I could no longer process as positive. The darkness had taken over so much of who I was, and I had become unreasonable—unreachable.

I slowly crept farther into the warm water toward the glowing horizon as the ache in my chest turned into sobs that poured out uncontrollably. Before I knew it, the water was just above my chest and starting to lap onto my face. I could no longer tell if it was the salt from my tears or the ocean I was tasting. In my heart, I knew there was no turning back, and I closed my eyes, held my breath, and started to go under.

One minute I was thinking, *I don't want to be here anymore*, and the next minute I'm back in my bed and it's the next morning. I know it sounds crazy, but I'm telling you the truth. That's honestly the miracle of it all. I don't know how I got from the water into my bed.

The last thing I remember thinking was *I'm done. I'm going to do this*, and then I woke up to the sounds of my daughter and wife downstairs, chatting and laughing with the friends we were staying with.

I sat up in bed, shocked with wet sand on the sheets. How had I gotten back here? I quietly got out of bed and went into the broom closet underneath the stairwell because I didn't want anybody to see me. I called my best friend and said, "I don't know what rock bottom looks like, but I'm pretty sure this is it," and I told him what had happened.

He started crying with me and then told me I needed to go talk to somebody. "You can't do this by yourself anymore, Jody." He put me in touch with a clinical psychologist near Nashville who I went to see when we returned home.

That beach trip was obviously dark and difficult. The beach is where my family goes when we need to escape the day-to-day stresses of life. It's a way to run away from home for a few days and get a fresh perspective. I had been in a deep depression in the months leading up to this particular trip. It was the end of a season that had been especially trying. I had lost a lot of weight because I quit eating, and I hadn't been sleeping well, either. I was falling apart emotionally and physically.

My perspective started to change the morning I woke up in that bed. After I made the phone call, I joined everyone in the kitchen and realized how close I had come to losing the people I love. I thought about what ending my life would have done to my sweet wife . . . my daughter.

Even now, it's hard to think about this almost-tragedy because a lot of people don't get this kind of second chance. They end up going through with it, and they leave behind a wake of heartache. My life's ambition since then—until my dying breath, which I hope is somewhere in my 90s—is to make sure that fewer people successfully end their own lives. We all have so many reasons to hold on, not the least of which are the people who depend on us.

I know my truth. There is no disillusionment, no fiction. My truth is that God did something miraculous to save my life in the waters of the Gulf of Mexico that night. In the weeks and months that followed, He did even more miraculous things to prove Himself to me and cement my calling in ways I never would have imagined.

Now it is my responsibility to share all He has done in my life with the hope that somehow it will make a marked difference in yours.

ONE:
THE MUSIC

s far back as my memory reaches, I always loved music. I grew up in church, but my parents encouraged me to listen to whatever music I liked. I was grateful they never said, "Oh, you can't listen to that!" Of course, when you're six, seven, or eight years old, you may have been listening to songs with questionable content but didn't even hear it half the time. You were just listening to it because you liked the beat, and it made you feel good.

The first record I ever owned was the *Grease* soundtrack. My parents had taken my brothers and me to the theater to see the movie, and I loved it. I sang along, totally clueless of how suggestive some of the lyrics were. Now as an adult, I listen back and I'm like, *Holy cow! Note to self: daughter cannot listen to "Greased Lightning."*

My mom's side of the family is from Spain, so a lot of the music she played at home was passionate and full of emotion.

She listened to Mario Lanza and Johnny Mathis. She loved listening to those lyric tenors with clear, high voices. She played their records all the time. As a kid, we listened to Johnny Mathis every Christmas. It wasn't Christmas without that warbly, tenor voice singing, "Sleigh bells ring, are you listening? In the lane . . ." Johnny had that special, high quality to his voice that made him unmistakable.

Even though I was around all this singing growing up, I never thought I was any good at it. As a matter of fact, I remember when I was around seven years old sitting in what we called the back-back-back of the car. We had a little Toyota hatchback, and I used to sit in the hatchback area and just roll around as we took the curves. (Obviously, this was way before seat belts or car seat laws.) My brother sat up front singing along to the radio while my mom drove. I overheard her say to him once, "You've got a really nice voice, Jimmy." Well, of course I wanted my mom to tell me *I* had a good voice, so I started singing along with the radio too.

My mom and my brother looked in the mirror at me as I sang along. They didn't say a word and even giggled a little. I thought, *They don't think I'm any good.* That night, I overheard my mom telling my dad, "Jody was singing along to the radio in the back of the car today. I think we've got a singer on our hands." From then on, and much to their irritation, I started singing along to everything.

Puberty didn't do much to change my voice. To this day, I still get called ma'am in the drive-through at Chick-fil-A. My wife and daughter think it's hilarious. I don't really care anymore, but when you're 18 years old and someone calls you ma'am, it can be irritating. I started feeling insecure and did everything I could to sing lower, cover my voice, and sound more like Michael McDonald as opposed to some chick.

I may have wanted to sound like a man, but growing up I listened to female singers, especially those with soul. I was a big fan of Aretha Franklin and Anita Baker, maybe because it was always easier for me to sing in their range, and I liked singing the high harmonies. My mom listened to Barbra Streisand, and I sang the harmony with her. I always felt my voice blended well with hers, but I wouldn't dare tell anybody for fear they'd beat me up.

That was in the '70s and '80s, and both my brothers were into rock 'n' roll. They were listening to bands like Queen and Kiss. Occasionally a Bee Gees or Air Supply song slid in because they were in the Top 40. When my brother listened to Kiss, I thought, *This music is awful. But wow! They can sing.* It wasn't necessarily my style of music, but I could appreciate the voices and what they were able to do with them. You have to admit that Freddie Mercury had a unique and incredible voice, as do Gene Simmons and Paul Stanley from Kiss.

I listened to Michael Jackson—the early Michael Jackson— and the Jackson 5. But if I'm honest, I'll have to admit that there was always something in Michael's voice that I found a little off-putting. Everybody liked Michael Jackson back in the late '70s and early '80s. He was just about as famous as you could be, and this was even before he dubbed himself the King of Pop. While I appreciated his production and his talent as an entertainer, I never could get on board with his voice and all the "tee-hee" stuff he did.

Back then, I don't think I ever thought, *Oh, when I grow up, I want to be a singer.* I just enjoyed singing. Every once in a while I sang in church, but I was terrified of people making fun of me and my high-pitched voice. People already called me Squeaky. I was also overweight when I was younger, so my middle brother (I get along great with him now) called me Blowdis or Blowdy instead of Jody because I was heavy. It did very little to encourage my self-esteem.

In addition to being self-conscious about my high voice, I was insecure about my weight. I'll never forget when I was 12 and my father took me to JCPenney to buy pants for school. He asked the salesperson for a medium husky. Husky? Seriously? Could we not find a better word, people? Needless to say, I was mortified.

I did everything I could to overcompensate for feeling different, awkward, and, if I'm honest, effeminate. I tried out for baseball teams and soccer teams in elementary and middle school, hoping it would help me fit in with other kids my age and even with my brothers. While I would have never admitted it back then, I'm comfortable now saying I didn't (and still don't) have very many athletic bones in my body. I love sports and enjoy watching just about all of them, but my skills were and are lacking when it came to implementation.

I ended up playing tennis in high school, but I wasn't very good at it. And anyway, tennis was never taken seriously as a man's man type of sport. (John McEnroe would probably beat me with his tennis racket if he heard me say that.) To this day, even my daughter pokes fun at me for playing tennis. While I didn't understand it or see it unfolding back then, all these experiences added to my gross insecurity.

My first real vocal solo was in fifth grade. Miss Hittinger was my teacher, and the school was having an end-of-the-year recital. She asked if anybody wanted to do a solo, and I raised my hand. I ended up singing the first verse of the song "Rainbow Connection" from *The Muppet Movie*. At the end, everybody clapped, and Miss Hittinger walked up to the microphone and said, "That was our very own Donny Osmond—Jody McBrayer. I've already told him that one day when he becomes a star, I get 25 percent of everything he makes." My father brought a small, cassette tape recorder with him that night to record the performance, and he and my mother must have listened to it a thousand times.

The next phase in my music life began when I was nine years old. That was the year my father became an ordained pastor. We were active in our local church, First Baptist Church in Riverview, Florida. They heard I could sing, and I was asked to sing in their youth musicals.

In my first musical, I played the role of a rooster (eye roll). It was the most famous rooster in all of Scripture (because there were so many)—the rooster that crowed when Peter denied Christ three times. I wore a ridiculous rooster costume, and evidently, I was really into my role, shaking my hips and strutting around the stage to one of the up-tempo songs at the Baptist Church.

It didn't take long before one of the church leaders pulled me aside during one of the rehearsals and said, "Hey, listen, you can't move like that, young man." It's not too common for pelvic-thrust dancing to happen onstage at any church, much less a Baptist Church. I told the man, "Okay," but then I just couldn't help it. It's how I felt the music, so I kept doing it.

Eventually, my parents told me just to stand there, sing, and only move my arms and hands. I tried. Honestly, I did, but that just didn't feel right to me. They ended up putting me behind a curtain so all you could see was my head with the rooster hat and beak. Even back then, the music was in me, and it was going to come out one way or another.

Our church had a Christmas pageant every year that was a pretty big deal in the community. They converted the parking lot into Bethlehem and erected a five-story scaffold where the heavenly host of angels was positioned. The head angel was lifted above them in a hydraulic bucket from a city electrical repair truck. I suppose someone at the church worked for the electric company. The scaffold was covered in greenery so the wood and metal structure wasn't seen. Lights aimed at the angels shone brightly, and music was piped through speakers in the trees. The scene was big and dramatic and actually quite beautiful, especially to a little kid.

Everybody wanted to be part of that pageant. There were no speaking lines; it was all narrated. I always wanted to play Joseph, but I was never picked for that part because I wasn't masculine enough, and I was also too chubby. No one told me that directly, but I overheard conversations that made it clear it wasn't ever going to happen. Instead, I always got stuck being a shepherd who was hiding—ahem—abiding in the field.

When Mary and Joseph entered the town on a donkey (we used a real donkey), they stopped at a well for water. One year I got to play the well boy and helped give them water. That was the organizers' way of throwing me a bone because I was one of the pastor's sons. I didn't realize it then, but it was just another example of learning how vulnerable we are to how people perceive us. Junk like this settles deep inside of you and only adds to how you feel about yourself. It shapes who you are at an early age. Instances like that made me wonder if something was wrong with me, no matter how trivial it seemed.

By the time I reached my double digits, the preteen years, my extracurriculars all had to do with music. I am now comfortable saying I'm not a super masculine guy. I no longer feel insecure about that, and I'm actually very happy with the person God made me. But during my junior high years, especially going through puberty, ugh! What a nightmare!

I have two older brothers who were both jocks. If there was a sport available in high school, they played it. Football, yes. Basketball, yes. Track, check. I even think one of them threw the shot put or the javelin, or something projectile in nature. They did it all.

I love them both so much, but it was intimidating for me to follow them into high school. Every coach looked at me and said, "Aren't you Richard and Jimmy's brother?" Their tone of voice telegraphed something like, "What the heck happened to you?" I didn't like myself at all as a freshman in high school. Then, when kids started throwing words at me like sissy, gay, or faggot, it broke me.

Even though most people didn't see me that way, or at least they never let on that they did, when people call you those names over and over again, you start to believe them. You begin asking if that's who you really are. To quote a line from the movie *Pretty Woman*, "The bad stuff is easier to believe." Sadly, that is true.

By the age of 12, I knew my voice was unique because when I sang, I saw people respond in a positive way. I watched them as they were emotionally moved by my voice. Many times, a person's first reaction when I opened my mouth to sing was surprise because I could actually carry a tune. Then I detected a change in their countenance as though my voice were a key and when I sang it unlocked something inside of them. I don't want this to sound like I'm bragging or being arrogant; that is most definitely not the message I'm sending here. I've just watched it happen time and time again. And at the age of 12, I didn't fully understand that this gift was actually the anointing of the Holy Spirit.

The family dynamic began shifting when they realized I had been gifted with a singing voice. Our dynamic was already unique because we were a blended family. My mother divorced when my brothers were three and five years old. While they knew their biological father, they didn't have a strong relationship with him. When my dad married my mom, he stepped in and took over raising them. He even tried to adopt them, but their biological father wouldn't let him. But Sonny McBrayer was their dad in the truest sense. He took both of them in and never looked back. That tells you a lot about the kind of person my father was. And it speaks volumes for my brothers because they never once considered him anything but their own dad. They wanted to call him Dad, but their biological father, who wasn't really present in their lives in any meaningful way, forbade it. So they called him Pop. When I was old enough, I called him Pop too.

Mom and Dad had me when my brothers were six and seven, so there's a pretty big age difference between us. Growing up, my brothers and I weren't all that close. My mother was obviously proud of how I sang. Even though my father was a strong supporter of everything I did, he was more involved in my brothers' sports, and my mom felt like my gifts were more up her alley.

Family and friends often came over for dinner or for the holidays, and Mom inevitably asked me to sing something. My brother Richard was always very verbal about not wanting to hear it. I think he was either embarrassed by it or embarrassed by me—maybe both. I don't think it was an issue of jealousy. He's a very secure person—well-built, tall, slender, dark hair, chiseled features, athletic. Deep down, I realize I always wanted Richard's approval. I wanted him to be proud of the person I was becoming and the gifts I had. Lord knows I was and am very proud of who he is.

Richard and I eventually had a conversation about it as adults. I explained that his negative reaction to my singing affected me in a real way. I'm not sure he understood, but I do believe he was sorry. He has never been a huge supporter of anything I've ever done professionally, although there have been small signs that maybe he was secretly proud of my music and accomplishments. Richard is a successful pharmaceutical rep, and he told me once that if a doctor says something about liking Christian music, he says, "Oh, my brother Jody was in the group Avalon."

It makes me happy to know we've gotten to the place where he is actually proud enough of me to claim me to someone else. Or maybe he's using me to sell pharmaceuticals. Either way, I suppose it's a step in the right direction. I've learned to not let it bother me anymore. When I was young, though, it hurt like hell and made me feel inferior. I had already been bombarded by those kinds of responses from people outside our family, so when it came from inside, it cut deeper. I always looked up to Richard and aspired to be at least half the man he was and is.

My parents were always supportive of me, but maybe it was because they saw my insecurities at such a young age. My dad's nickname for me was Butch. I mean, I couldn't have been more the opposite of a Butch, but he called me that since I was old enough to remember. I think he knew I was going to be different in a lot of ways from my brothers.

He never treated me any differently than the other two boys. Since I was the baby of the family, my parents spent a lot more money on me once my brothers moved out of the house, and I might have had a couple extra polo shirts in the closet. My dad worked as hard as he could for all of us.

My parents were fantastic about supporting my growing love for singing and music. My mom was the one who pushed me artistically, not because my dad wasn't great at it but because he couldn't carry a tune in a bucket. The arts were definitely my mom's territory. I have to give my mom credit; she's responsible for not letting me be lazy when I sang. One of the key pieces of being a good singer actually has nothing to do with singing; it's about communication. It's important to make a connection with the listener.

I remember talking to my friend Mark Lowry about singers. He was comparing two amazing tenor singers, both strong in their own right. He said, "One of them sings the notes; the other one sings the song." What he meant and what my mom understood was that you can be the most amazing singer in the world and hit every note, but if you don't pour your heart into it and communicate the song, it's pointless.

My mom pushed me from being just a singer to being a real communicator. I would sit in our living room singing into a hairbrush, and my mom would say, "You know, if you're singing it but you don't believe it, then there's no point in singing. You're not going to move anybody. You have to sing it and believe the words."

How much could an eight-year-old kid understand about lyrics such as "Wise men say, only fools rush in, but I can't help falling in love with you"? It's hard to pull from a well of experience you don't have, but a good singer knows this is essential, so even if you don't understand a song's meaning personally, you have to at least try to empathize when you're singing it.

My mother also wanted me to take piano lessons. I tried but quit after the second or third lesson because, well, I hated it. I regret it, for sure, because it would have made things much easier for me later in my career. I can play enough to write a tune, but I don't play well enough to not have to depend on somebody else to accompany me. In some ways, I like that because I have the freedom to not be stuck behind a piano.

My mom said to me, "Well, if you won't take piano, will you at least take voice lessons?" I agreed, and at 12, I started taking voice lessons from an older woman named Eugenia Halston. Trust me, she was as eccentric as her name sounds. She always wore lace, high-collar dresses and a flower brooch. Remember, we lived in Florida where it's about 106 degrees in the winter, but without fail she'd wear her signature outfit. The first time I met her, I seriously wondered what my mother had gotten me into.

Eugenia was a kind, gentle lady, and coincidentally, she was also the piano player at the program where I sang my first solo in elementary school. Her husband was a retired army general, and they lived around the corner from us on the river. She was a thin woman, but for some reason, she had really fat fingers, especially her thumb. I watched her play the piano and was always amazed that she could play with those thumbs. They were shaped like clubs. She wore a diamond ring, and when she played, it clicked on the keys the entire time. The stone was huge, and I always imagined it flying out of that ring, soaring across the room, and hitting me in the eye.

Around that time, my father bought an old Vespa scooter at a garage sale, much to my mother's disdain. He fixed up the little motor scooter enough for it to start and run. Every Monday, Wednesday, and Friday when I came home from school, I hopped on that Vespa and drove around the corner about a mile or so to my voice teacher's house.

Eugenia had attended the Juilliard School of Music when she was young. She was trained in classical piano as well as vocal performance. While she had more piano students than vocal students, vocal pedagogy was something she was passionate about and was the reason she took me on as a student. Until I started taking lessons from her, I had no idea about the vast world of music or what it meant to be classically trained.

Within a couple of months, Eugenia taught me how to sing in Italian as well as German. While she was kind, she was also a stoic woman and did things by the book. She was never rude and always well-mannered, but she wasn't what I'd describe as a warm person. However, I think I softened her up inadvertently.

As I've already pointed out, I was a chubby kid, or the preferred term at my age was *husky*, so at my first lesson, I walked in, said hello, and asked if she had any snacks. (It was after school, and I was hungry.) She seemed both surprised and slightly put out by that question. Her husband had turned their garage into a little studio with a piano, a small stage, and all her music stuff. The entrance was on the side of the garage, and I don't think she ever expected her students to come into her main home. When I asked her for snacks, she told me to come into the kitchen and she would find something.

She gave me peanut butter crackers and Kool-Aid. (I was all about the Kool-Aid.) While I was eating, she told me she'd never had a student ask her for food before a lesson, which, from what I can remember, had no bearing on my asking for or enjoying the snack. Every lesson after that, I came in and she said, "Let's go have your snack, and then we'll get to work." I think my cute, husky self won her over.

Eugenia deserves a huge amount of credit for bringing me out of my shell and telling me to be okay with my high voice. She also taught me about classical music and the importance of learning it as a foundation. She took her piano and voice students to a couple competitions and also put on a big recital in downtown Tampa. That recital was the first time I had ever sung a song in another language. I can still sing every word of that song to this day.

Eugenia gave me lessons for two years, and then she got ill and couldn't teach anymore. She was upset that our lessons had to end. At my final recital with her, she accompanied me on the piano for two songs: "Who'll Buy My Lavender?" written by English composer Edward German in 1896 and an Italian song,

"La Donna è Mobile." I loved singing them both even though neither made any sense to me. As I sang, she wept at the piano. I couldn't understand why she was crying, but afterward she put her arm around me and said, "I can't wait to see what God's going to do with you. You have a true gift, and it's been an honor to teach you."

That was the last time I saw her. She became very ill and passed away several years later. The lessons she taught me as a young boy will stay with me forever, as well as my love for peanut butter crackers and Kool-Aid.

TWO:
THE PREACHER

When I was eight years old, my dad was called to the ministry. When the calling hit him, it hit him hard and fast. He dove in headfirst and never stopped to evaluate the toll it would take on him or his family. He just knew deep in his heart that he was called to be a pastor.

After he was ordained, he took a part-time position as a preacher of a small church, where he served for about four years and then served as youth pastor for another four years. It almost ate him and my mother alive. When he left the lead pastor position and decided to become the youth pastor, he said it was because he could relate better to teenagers. He used to say, "Teenagers are so much nicer than adults . . . and way more fun."

My pop was truly an amazing example of Christ both in my life and in countless others'. He also worked full-time for the US Postal Service as a letter carrier and then became a postmaster toward the end of his life. During his letter-carrier years, he woke before the sun came up and was gone before any of us got up for school. Back then, postal workers had horrible hours and had to go in early to sort all the mail by hand for their route.

One of my fondest memories was waking up early in the morning to use the bathroom and looking into the kitchen and seeing my father kneeling by a kitchen chair, his face buried in his hands, praying out loud for his family. At the time, I didn't understand how significant that simple act of faithfulness was. Now, as an adult, I can only hope to be as strong on my feet as he was on his weak, arthritic knees.

Growing up, I watched the ins and outs of ministry take its toll on my parents. My dad got phone calls, sometimes at 3:00 in the morning, from people he pastored in the inner city of Tampa. Those middle-of-the-night calls were from people who had just lost their mother or who were in abusive situations. My dad would get in his car and drive 45 minutes to be there for them. Keep in mind that he wasn't making a lot of money. He was basically a part-time pastor being paid far less than a part-time salary. That's just the kind of heart he had.

Since I grew up as the pastor's kid in a fundamental Baptist church, it was easy to think of God as a velvet-covered hammer. There were a lot of rules, but my parents were pretty relaxed. My father was a cusser, a habit he developed from his time in the air force. He also had an occasional beer—he wasn't a drinker by any stretch—but he was a real person who didn't feel the pressure to be inauthentic.

My dad believed in a code for how you should live life. Be fair, honest, and truthful, and treat people the way you want to be treated. Love others as much as possible. He taught me that if you see a person asking for money on the street, give them money regardless of what you feel or think, and let God work out the details. He used to say, "The Bible says we're supposed to help widows and orphans and people in need, no questions asked."

I saw these qualities in both my parents, but I was also surrounded by legalism and people sending a different message. Because my father was on staff at church, I felt pressured to be what everybody expected me to be. My brothers were already out of the house, so anytime we went on youth trips for kids who were at least 15, I was always the youngest. Naturally, I didn't fit in with that older crowd, so I was a sort of tagalong kid who was there because my dad was the youth pastor. People were nice to me, nobody was ever mean, and I had a great core group of friends at church, but I always felt like an outsider.

I never felt like I fit in to the church mold because I was always super-independent and had a bit of foolishness and rebellion at my core. I cut up and did stupid things and then got in trouble. For instance, I could never keep a straight face in church. The moment it was time to be quiet, the smallest thing became hilarious. My friends made me laugh all the time because I had a snort I couldn't control. My father knew it was me and made that *tsk* sound and then threw me a dirty look, which shut me up for at least the rest of the sermon.

It was difficult for me because being the irreverent one made me think I couldn't be good. I had that rebellious spirit they talked about in Sunday school. For the record, I never did anything *really* bad, just stupid kid things, like the time one of my friends brought a BB gun to church in the back of his dad's truck. Remember, we were in Riverview, Florida, which back in the day was as red as you could get. I mean, he brought a BB gun to church, for Pete's sake! My friend said, "Let's go shoot some squirrels." I was down with that, anything to not have to sit through the service. So we went around the church grounds and shot some random stuff.

There was an old woman whose property backed up to the rear of the church property. We came up on her house and saw she had an exposed pipe that ran out of her house and into the ground. My friend said, "I'll bet you can't hit that pipe." I'm pretty certain I didn't even blink. I just shot, and before I knew it, there was water spraying out of the pipe. The lady must have been washing dishes or something because she immediately came out back and saw us running. I distinctly remember hearing her say, "Jody McBrayer, I see you, and I'm gonna tell your daddy!" How was I supposed to know she was the church secretary? And for that matter, why wasn't she in church? (Ahem . . . backslider.)

Needless to say, I got in big trouble for that one. I had to pay to repair the pipe with my allowance. My dad didn't have to spank me; his disappointed look was enough to get his point across.

When my father was called to the ministry, my mother reluctantly came along. She was supportive of his work and never pushed back when he wasn't home or when he had to work long hours. The first church my dad was assigned to, the one in the inner city, was a cinder block rectangle with windows. By the time my dad's assignment there ended, my mom had made it beautiful. She put some stained-glass art on the walls, had the place carpeted, and had a group bring in new pews. She made the choir loft look nice and hung curtains on the windows. That's what my mom's giftings were. She also has the gift of hospitality, so she often helped with the food and special events in the fellowship hall.

I never heard her complain about any of it, but I don't think she ever loved being a pastor's wife. She was better once my dad became a youth pastor because it was in our home church where she had friends. She traveled with my dad and helped with the youth activities, which was more her thing.

Spending all those years in church, you know there had to be some funny stories, and I can't let all this talk about church end without telling a couple of them. As I've already mentioned, my dad was the youth pastor at our home church where I was baptized. The pastor and my dad were friends. They went through several associate pastors, and one of them was a Chinese man with a unique sense of humor—and unique social etiquette.

My parents often invited him to dinner or went out to dinner with him after the service. It was common for him to literally belch and pass gas at the table without so much as an "excuse me" or "I'm sorry." If you think it can't get any worse, he also picked his nose and wiped it on his napkin in front of everyone, spoiling appetites one booger, belch, and fart at a time.

Part of the associate pastor's job in the church was being responsible for the lit signage in front of the church. People get pretty creative with these messages, and sometimes they're biblical expressions or a play on words related to Scripture. In 1976, there was a popular ad campaign slogan for Peter Pan peanut butter. It said, "If you believe in peanut butter, you've got to believe in Peter Pan."

In hindsight, I don't know what belief had to do with peanut butter or how this helped advertise said product, but whatever. Because it was so popular, the assistant pastor put the following on the sign outside the church: "If you believe in peanut butter, you've got to believe in Jesus Christ," which made absolutely no sense at all. My dad said a number of times as we passed by the church sign, "That's the dumbest thing I've ever read in my life."

So my parents decided to do something about it. In the dark of night, my father and mother dressed in black and loaded a ladder onto their car. They drove to the church, climbed the ladder, and changed the sign. They covered up the words *Jesus Christ* and replaced it with the words *Peter Pan*.

I wish I could tell you that everyone found the joke hilarious. Not so. You would have thought that hell had frozen over because the next day people were very upset that somebody had covered up the name Jesus Christ and changed it to Peter Pan. They wanted to file a police report and find out who the guilty party was. My father was in every meeting regarding the atrocity and just shook his head and agreed how horrible it all was. He acted shocked and appalled that anyone would ever do such a thing. I think this made it funnier than the actual act of changing the sign.

That was the kind of thing my dad did because he had a sense of humor, which some at church considered irreverent and unacceptable. I inherited that sense of humor, which will explain a lot of my later story. My father ended up telling the lead pastor that he was the one who changed the sign. The pastor also thought it was funny but asked my dad not to do it again because people were far too offended.

Here's another funny story about when my dad worked at this small Baptist church. As most of you know, vacation Bible school (VBS) has always been a big deal and a strong outreach for churches. My mom volunteered at VBS, and I went with her to help out. There was always snack time, and in order to make enough Kool-Aid for the number of kids who came, they used giant, stainless-steel vats to mix it and serve the kids. The vats were so deep that there was no good way to stir the mix because the spoon handles weren't long enough to reach the bottom. However, the kitchen lady had a workaround for this problem.

If I had not witnessed it with my own eyes, I wouldn't have believed it. She rolled up her sleeve and stuck her entire arm into the container, past her elbow, and stirred, mixing the powder with the water. My mom came home from volunteering one day and said to me, "Under no circumstances are you to drink the Kool-Aid, do you understand?" I asked her why (because, as you know, I really liked Kool-Aid). "Just trust me, you don't want it." My father used to call that kitchen lady Old Red Arm.

Okay, one more story and then I promise I'm done. A few years ago, I was in Gatlinburg, Tennessee, with Avalon. We were doing an event for LifeWay, and my wife, daughter, and I were staying in a hotel. Standing on the balcony and looking up the hill, I saw the hotel where I had stayed for summer camp when I was a kid. It's a large, round hotel that sits on a hill that overlooks all of Gatlinburg. I was so excited to go to summer camp there. Once again, it was one of those situations where I was too young to go but because my father was the youth pastor, I went. The summer camp was organized by the Southern Baptist Convention with invitations going out to all Southern Baptist youth groups to attend this well-planned event in a brand-new hotel. Thousands of teenagers from dozens of churches showed up.

I'm hesitant to say it, but *thank God* things have changed since then. This youth retreat was planned more like a senior citizens' retreat. The entertainment scheduled for 5,000 teenagers was Miss Alabama, who also happened to be a classically trained opera singer. After her performance was a series of mind-numbing speakers sure to slip the most caffeinated young person into a coma. There were no fun activities, just opera and preaching. By the second day, everyone wanted to leave, including my father.

Finally, about midway through the week, my father decided to escape with the youth group from our church. We loaded up our bus after breakfast and drove to the mountains to find an empty spot where we could have worship time and Bible study. It ended up being one of the sweetest and most memorable moments of his entire time as a youth pastor.

For the rest of the retreat, my father and the other youth leaders kept their own agenda every day instead of the planned camp schedule. We had some amazing days before coming back to the hotel for some R&R. One day after we came back, a couple of the boys from our group decided to spend some time in the hot tub. Somehow they managed to sneak an entire bottle of Dawn dishwashing detergent into the hot tub with them. You probably know where this is going.

My balcony overlooked the hot tub that emptied into the swimming pool. I looked over and wasn't able to make out where the pool and hot tub were since the suds were so thick. There were giant soap sud shapes floating down the hill and into the city of Gatlinburg. The wind carried off a large conglomeration of bubbles, and we all sat back and tried to make out what each shape looked like. I'm pretty sure one of them looked exactly like a fully formed unicorn. There were *a lot* of bubbles.

It was the day before the camp was supposed to end, but given this small inconvenience and the fact that we hadn't been around for a few days, both the hotel and the convention asked us to pack up and leave. It was slightly awkward walking through the lobby to the bus as everyone watched. If my father was nervous about coming home early after being shamed by the Southern Baptist Convention, he never showed it. I can't imagine what went through his mind as he drove home. Obviously, he was trying to come up with the best way to explain to the church and the parents why summer camp got cut short.

The following Sunday when the youth got up and spoke about the retreat and what they had learned, there wasn't a dry eye in the place. God had worked in a strong way, and many hearts were changed during that trip. No one even cared about the soap suds debacle, and then we went so far as to name our church buses Sudsie and Sudsie II. The youth department grew exponentially after that because the kids needed an outlet, and they knew if they came to youth group, it wasn't going to be stiff and boring. They realized it was a place where they could let their hair down and just be who they are.

* * *

Even though I was raised in the church, I didn't decide to accept Christ until I was 16. My dad was the one who led me to the Lord after a youth event one Monday night. We called it Youth Explosion, which sounds so cheesy now, but it was a thriving youth group, and everyone looked forward to Monday nights.

I had just gotten my driver's license and had driven my father to church for the meeting. That night, we had a special speaker, and afterward, a bunch of teens came forward to accept Christ. I watched them, thinking for the first time that something was missing in my own life. On the drive home, I was quiet, partly because I was still concentrating on driving a five-speed but also because I was thinking about why I had never made the decision to accept Christ after being surrounded by it my entire life. My dad asked me if I was okay. I told him what was on my mind.

"Well, you did go down to the front when you were younger," he said.

"Pop, I was five years old. I don't even remember it, much less what it meant."

"Well, why don't we take care of that when we get home?"

My father came into my room just before I went to sleep, and we knelt beside my bed. I remember being eye-level with Chew-

27

bacca and the Millennium Falcon, realizing even then that I was probably too old to still be sleeping on *Star Wars* sheets. My dad asked me why I wanted to become a Christian. "Because I know that following Christ is the right thing to do," I answered. "I want to live my life for Christ." So we bowed our heads, and he walked me through a prayer. That night, without question, I knew I had become a Christian. It's one of the most memorable moments of my life—so vivid and clear in my mind. I will be forever grateful that I got to share that moment with my dad.

THREE:
THE CALLING

By the time I was a senior in high school, I knew that music was something I wanted to pursue. I started singing in the school ensemble and the youth choir at church, and I also decided to try musical theater.

I auditioned for the senior musical because one of my best friends was trying out, and he wanted me to come along. I was already struggling with the stigma that music carried with it and apprehension about taking that leap into musical theater. Anyone who did anything other than sports was considered a sissy in those days. There was also the issue of my higher-pitched voice and being less masculine.

The musical was *Oklahoma!* and the drama teacher asked me to try out for the part of Curly, the lead part. I sang from the opening number. "Oh, what a beautiful mornin', oh, what a beautiful day. I've got a beautiful feelin' everything's goin' my way." There were a couple of other guys auditioning, so I didn't think I would get the part. Deep down, there was a part of me that hoped I wouldn't. The term *sissy* was thankfully fading from use, and now that I was a senior, people were becoming more accepting of me, but I didn't want to add fuel to what seemed to be a smoldering fire.

I was blessed to get along with just about everyone, but of course, there were always bullies who made smart remarks, called me a queer or a fag, simply because I didn't play football. Those characters will always be there, even in adulthood.

A couple of days later, I found out I had landed the lead role of Curly.

I had mixed feelings about getting the part. I felt anxious and self-conscious singing and performing musical theater because I didn't want the stigma that came along with it, but when I was actually doing it, I had so much joy. When many of my classmates and even some of the bullies heard me sing, they said, "Wow, this isn't just a guy who likes to sing. He's good!"

It was during my senior year between the musical and all the other fine arts projects I was involved in that I realized I was actually a decent singer and that it was something I enjoyed doing. During the rehearsals for *Oklahoma!* I thought, *This is a lot of fun.* The girl who played the part of Laurey, Curly's love interest, was a girl named Kim who was beautiful *and* a phenomenal singer. I had a crush on her, and in one scene, we had to kiss. Needless to say, as a 17-year-old boy, I looked forward to that scene every rehearsal and every performance. But beyond just the kissing scene, I loved every minute of being onstage.

Even though I was also involved with a lot of music at my church, it hadn't crossed my mind or my heart for that matter that maybe God was going to call me to do Christian music as a full-time ministry.

* * *

Riverview, Florida, is about an hour from Orlando, and my family used to drive to Disney World a lot. I loved (and still love) everything Disney. Every year at the Magic Kingdom, there was an event called Night of Joy where they shut the park down to the general public at 5:00 p.m. and reopened at 7:30 p.m. for Night of Joy ticket holders. Popular Christian artists played on stages all over the park until 1:00 in the morning. The cost was about $50 (this was in the late '80s, and it would probably cost about $1,000 today). You got to hear all your favorite Christian artists, ride all the rides, and see all the attractions, and the crowds weren't as crazy as a normal Disney visit. Our church took busloads there almost every year.

I went to Night of Joy three or four times as a teenager. I confess that I was more excited about being at Disney World than I was about seeing any of the Christian artists. At Disney World, I felt transported to another place and time. Even when I was old enough to drive, my friends and I drove there during the summer and on weekends and had a blast. When I was finally able to share it with my own daughter, it was a true highlight as a parent.

I went to Night of Joy in 1988, my senior year in high school. I was particularly excited about it because even though I wasn't a huge Christian music fan, I actually loved Christian artist Amy Grant. She had just released her greatest hits collection called *The Collection*. There was a song on that record called "Stay for a While" that we played over and over while we drove to Orlando. In that moment, I thought that song was the best song I had ever heard in my life. It felt so fresh, energetic, and different from anything I had ever heard before, especially in Christian music.

That night at Walt Disney World was a pivotal life moment for me. As we stood in front of Cinderella Castle, one of my favorite places in the world, Amy Grant took the stage. I just stood there in awe—probably experiencing sensory and emotional overload. Time seemed to slow down, and I watched her, thinking, *One day, I'm going to do that.*

I'm not sure there was a whole lot of spirituality involved in my decision to pursue a career in Christian music. I was just a kid who wanted to do that thing I saw onstage. I didn't know how I was going to accomplish it, but I just knew that one day I was going to make it happen. I wish I could say I was prayerfully petitioning God to give me the chance to fulfill my calling, but I didn't have that kind of spiritual maturity at that point. It wasn't that I didn't have strong, spiritual influences in my life during that time; it's obvious to me now that God was putting things in order to fulfill His purpose.

My family was close friends with another family, Russ and Jill Amerling and their daughters, Kim and Karen. Russ and Jill were my godparents, and they came over every Christmas morning after breakfast and spent Christmas Day with us. We went on camping trips and vacations together, and all of them were very involved helping my father in the youth ministry at our church. They were like my second parents in a lot of ways. (Interesting side note: Russ and Jill are the people responsible for the Choose Life license plate campaign. They started the initiative in the state of Florida, and it has spread to almost every US state.)

Near the end of my senior year, I sang in church one Sunday morning, and afterward, Kim Amerling encouraged me to go hear a Christian music group called TRUTH that was performing in Lakeland, about an hour from where we lived. She knew I had a growing interest in singing. So my parents and I piled into our station wagon and drove an hour to Carpenter's Home Church. The church was *huge*—nearly 10,000 seats right in the middle of central Florida. At the time, it was also the home of the only Christian radio station in our area, WCIE.

We arrived late, and the concert had already started. The floor of the auditorium was packed, and I remember walking in and seeing people excited, clapping, worshipping, and engaged with what was happening onstage. As I listened, I became overwhelmed with how good those singers were and how they moved together in such a professional way. It was like nothing I had ever seen before, especially for Christian music.

The male singers in the group—Marty Magehee, Mark Harris, Andy Chrisman, and Kirk Sullivan—were incredible with soulful, strong, commanding voices. (These guys would eventually leave TRUTH to form the popular contemporary Christian music (CCM) group 4Him.) I had no idea that kind of music and presentation was possible unless you were a superstar like Amy Grant or Michael W. Smith.

I kept noticing a guy walking around behind everyone onstage. He was behind the singers and in front of the band just flailing his arms or standing back with them folded, looking at the singers and band approvingly. I assumed he was directing, but I wasn't quite sure. It looked more like random pointing and moments of pensive thinking than it did directing. After several songs, he took the microphone and began to speak. He said his name was Roger Breland and that he was the founder and director of TRUTH. Now the random pointing made a little more sense, kind of.

There was a moment in the middle of that concert that I will never forget. The group was singing a song called "There

Is a Hope," and, with tears in my eyes, I looked up at my dad and said, "I think this is what I'm supposed to do." That was the first time it went beyond just singing and performing. I knew there was more to it than that. The Holy Spirit was strong in that church that evening, and all I knew was that I wanted to be part of what He was doing. That was the moment that everything changed for me. It went from "I want to be a star" to "Okay, maybe God is in this," at least as much as I could understand it at that point in my life.

That night, God planted something in my heart as I sat there watching TRUTH. I could feel the power in the music. The anointing that was filling the room was strong. The message was making a visceral connection with the audience and changing the hearts and feelings of the people in the space. I knew because it was happening with me . . . with my parents. I was in awe watching how the crowd responded to it.

Growing up Baptist, I hadn't been in a church where people raised their hands and responded to the music the way these people were responding, and it didn't scare me at all. Remember how I mentioned earlier that I was able to watch people change physically as I sang? Well, that's what was happening in this room when this group sang, and it was happening to me.

What I witnessed that night at the TRUTH concert was completely different from what happened at Night of Joy. It was a completely different experience. On this night, people were crying, raising their hands, going forward, and asking for prayer. I thought, *This is what music is supposed to do.*

When I looked up at my dad during that concert and told him that was what I wanted to do, I do not recall his exact response, but it was something like, "I have no doubt this is who you were created to be." I believe he knew this way before I did, and that's probably why he didn't skip a beat. He took my hand and walked me down the aisle to the front where all those people were praying. He and the director locked eyes, and my dad literally grabbed Roger Breland's pant leg, pulled on it, and said, "My son wants to sing in this group. How would he do that?"

Roger looked at him and then looked at me and said, "Well, how old is your son?" My dad told him I was 17. Roger knelt down by us and told my dad that I needed to go to college first and get some life experience and an education. My dad asked, "Any suggestions as to where he should go?" Roger said, "My sons are going to Liberty University. It's a great Christian school. Maybe you should look into it. They have music programs there, and if your son can sing, that's a great place for him to get experience." My dad thanked him, Roger shook both our hands, and we walked back to our seats.

I cried the entire ride home. I didn't even know why I was crying. I just knew that something bigger was at work, and I couldn't explain it. I think my mom and dad knew it too. All my father talked about on the ride home was getting in touch with Liberty University and taking that next step—college. All I could think about was, *Where the heck is Liberty University?*

I was terrified at the idea of going to college. I didn't know what I was going to do there. I was an okay student in high school, but the idea of going away to college and being far from home, my family, and my friends was overwhelming. The only thing I knew for sure now was that I had to go.

A week after the concert, my dad called Liberty University and somehow tracked down the secretary for the head of the music department. She was very kind and informative and told us that a Liberty University ensemble group called the Sounds of Liberty was going to be in our area in the coming weeks.

My dad said, "Hey, my son went to a TRUTH concert recently, and Liberty was recommended to him. He's a singer, and I'm wondering what it would take for him to get an audition." The secretary told him they didn't normally audition freshmen. She said that Boss (what they called the head of the music department) and Dr. David Randlett, the head of the School of Music, usually recommend that students attend school for a year before auditioning. As sophomores, they can get on a list to audition for one of several ensembles on campus. "Chances are he won't make Sounds because they are considered the premier ensemble," she said. "Being accepted to that group is difficult and typically not open to freshmen."

As the secretary continued to talk, Dr. Randlett came into her office and happened to overhear her conversation. He told her, "Tell him to come to our concert in Dunedin, Florida, and I'll let him sing. But we don't accept freshmen."

A month later in Dunedin, we arrived late (that seemed to be a pattern for us) but got to hear the last couple of songs. After the concert, Dr. Randlett came up to us and introduced himself. He put me onstage and made me sing "His Eye Is on the Sparrow" while the group was tearing down equipment and the audience was leaving the church.

I was a nervous wreck and not sure I sang my best. When it was over, Dr. Randlett came over to me and said, "Just so you know, being in the Sounds of Liberty requires you to stay at school during the summer for seven weeks and work at Thomas Road Baptist Church. We travel with Jerry Falwell and sing at any events he requires us to. It is a lot of work, but it does come with a full scholarship. If you get selected, you'll be one of the first freshmen to ever join the group. We'll be in touch and let you know."

We waited and waited and waited. I applied to other schools and was actually accepted to a couple of them, but they didn't offer scholarships. We were holding out for Liberty, but the time was getting tight. My high school graduation was a month away, and I had to make a decision. I didn't know what I was going to do.

One afternoon when I was in my ensemble class at school, my dad walked into the classroom, threw his hands up over his head, and with tears in his eyes said, "We made it, buddy! You did it," and he gave me one of his million-dollar hugs. Back then, a full ride meant a $75,000 scholarship. I don't know that I've ever seen him prouder than he was when he gave me that news, except maybe on my wedding day.

At my high school graduation, it was customary to have students who had been awarded scholarships stand and announce the name of the college they would be attending and the amount of their scholarship. When my turn came, I stood up, and someone said, "Jody McBrayer, Liberty University, full ride, $75,000 scholarship, School of Music."

People gasped at the announcement, and it began to dawn on me that this must be a big deal. I had no idea what the cost of college was until I was awarded that scholarship. My family was huge University of Florida supporters, and I always thought (and I think my father hoped) I would be a Gator. When I asked my dad if he was disappointed that I wasn't going to be part of the Gator Nation, his response was, "I love the Gators, but free school is better."

FOUR:
THE BETRAYED

While I was settling in at college, a lot was going on at my home church. One particular situation caused a great deal of strife for my dad and our family's relationship with the church.

The senior pastor at the church where my dad served as youth pastor was Ben Earnest. He was one of my dad's closest friends and a truly amazing man. He actually led my mom and dad to the Lord. He baptized them and then me when I was five years old.

He was a little older than my parents and decided to retire when he was in his mid-70s. He became the church's pastor emeritus. The church then put together a pastor search committee to try to find a new pastor to replace him. Sadly, when you put something together by committee, it's usually like being on the wrong side of a firing squad—it never ends well.

After an exhaustive search and a few possible candidates interviewed, the church finally found a man they wanted to hire.

Everyone on the search committee was swooning over him—everyone but my father. He said there was just something not right, that something felt "off" with him.

My dad looked into the guy's past and found that he had lied to the search committee about his credentials. Surprisingly, no one checked to see if any of it was true. Wanting to be honest with the committee, my dad told them he felt like hiring the man was a mistake. Dad tried to press his case, but they didn't want to hear it. They told him it was none of his business and that he was overstepping. This decision started to divide the congregation. People my family had considered friends for years turned against my dad. It got so bad that my father stepped down from his role as youth pastor.

We're taught that Christ is enough, and I absolutely believe that He is enough for every need we will ever have. However, we were created for fellowship; we were created for *koinonia*, for that fellowship with other believers to build up one another, to find like-minded people to share our lives with. When it all fell apart, I watched people my dad had loved for years turn their back on him.

I'm not sure my dad knew how to deal with that because he was sincerely not the kind of person who would ever do that to someone. If anyone was made for fellowship with others, it was my dad. But another quality about him was that he stood up for what he believed was right. He wasn't afraid to rock the boat if he saw something unjust happening, another trait I most definitely got from him.

It damaged the trust my mom and dad had in people and the church in general. Even though I was at Liberty when all this went down, it planted in me a seed of mistrust for the church too.

Although my dad was working part-time as a youth pastor, anyone in ministry knows there's no such thing as a part-time pastor. Oh, they'll pay you part-time but expect you to be there every minute the doors are open, which is fine since that's the nature of working in ministry. But I say this to make the point that my dad was tired emotionally and physically. After going through what we perceived as a betrayal, he decided to walk away from what had become a full-time ministry.

My parents didn't go back to church for a long time after that. I actually don't know if my father ever darkened the doors of a church on Sunday morning again unless it was to hear me sing. His heart was broken. But I want this point to be clear: my parents may have left the church, but I don't believe my father ever lost his faith in Christ. He just lost his faith in people. It was difficult to witness. He had poured all his energy, love, and time into serving the members of our church, and he watched those same people throw it all back in his face, all because they couldn't admit they were wrong.

This made me bitter with the church for a while. It made me question a lot about what the church was doing and if they were even doing it right. I started asking questions that, especially back then, were considered taboo. Church was not a place to ask questions. There was no tolerance for disagreement. The message was to be good, tithe, and keep quiet. I was never very good at following at least two of those. I'll let you figure out which two. Here's a hint, it's not tithing.

When my dad passed, a lot of people from the congregation came to his funeral. Many told me and my family that they regretted so much of what had happened. The pastor the church hired ended up leaving after a short time. Much of what my father had warned them about and more came to the surface, and those responsible for his hiring had to come to grips with the mistakes they had made.

I was angry with that pastor for what he had allowed to happen and for the lies he had told. He knowingly let my father leave the church and the ministry, losing lifelong friendships in the process, and did nothing to stop any of it. Interestingly—and true to form—

that pastor and his wife showed up at an Avalon concert several years later, all smiles and gushing, wanting backstage passes and special treatment. I thought, *You've got a lot of nerve showing up after what you did to my parents.* I didn't actually say that to him, but God knows I wanted to. I made sure they got their tickets and passes and met the group, and I put on a happy face because my father asked me to. Pop always chose the high road and treated people with kindness, even if it wasn't reciprocated. I have to say, this quality doesn't come as easily for me. I have a penchant for seeing people get what they deserve when they've treated others poorly. My father always said, "Nobody can get them back like Jesus can. Be kind, and let Him sort it out."

As I mentioned, I was at Liberty during this time. Coincidentally, the pastor my dad was skeptical about told me his roommate in seminary was one of my professors. I decided to ask my professor about it. "I've never heard of that person in my life," my professor said. I told my dad. The next time my dad came to Lynchburg, he asked the professor himself, thinking surely he'd remember a roommate. He did not.

It may have been obvious to us during the interview process that this pastor wasn't being honest, but it wasn't to everyone else. He was very sharp, well-dressed, and sophisticated, and the search committee liked that because we were just a little country church. Maybe they thought he would somehow class the place up. The sad part is that the church was thriving and amazing the way it was, and this man did a lot to stifle growth in the short time he was there. The people who had selected him just sat back and let it happen rather than admit they had made a mistake. Pride can be an ugly, destructive thing.

Sadly, this kind of thing happens in churches a lot. Church politics can be destructive. I've watched disagreements and division slowly eat away at my friends and the people I love who serve as worship pastors and senior pastors of churches. It's like a cancer. When a church is unhealthy and has an unstable foundation and a pastor has no accountability, the negative fallout is larger than any positive work the church is trying to accomplish for Christ.

I'm in no way anti-church. However, as my friend Roger Breland says, "I think sometimes God looks down at churches on Sunday mornings and says, 'Don't blame any of this mess on Me.'"

Both the problem with and the wonderful part about church is that it's made up of human beings—flawed, destructive, difficult, obstinate, beautiful, creative, talented, wonderful people. I've observed that people who don't have any kind of status or position of authority in their life, maybe they earn a minimum wage paycheck at a thankless job with little recognition, become the head deacon of their church or head elder or, even worse, the lead pastor. All of a sudden, they have a little bit of power. If their heart is not in the right place, that power can be misconstrued or abused.

I've seen it a thousand times, but for every thousand I've seen, I've seen two thousand times where people's lives have been changed by amazing moments in church. There is power when God's people come together and encourage one another. That's what the church is about. The church is the people. When people come together in a place where they can help one another, build up one another, and bear each other's burdens, the whole body of Christ gets healed and strengthened. Then, and only then, can we go out and tell the world about Christ.

Over the years, I watched my dad love on people who the church wasn't very good at loving. At his memorial service after he passed away, the church was full of the kids from his youth group who were now adults. They came back with their families to honor him. People came up to me after the service and said,

"You know, your dad changed my life. He loved me when no one else did. He was like a second father to me." Another person said, "Your dad took me in and showed me Christ when nobody else had any patience for me. He took his time and never gave up on me." He changed the lives of a lot of teens in ways I'm not sure anyone realized. I feel certain that his reward in heaven is vast and that he is seeing the fruits of all his labor and sacrifice.

That's just the kind of guy he was. For all the amazing ministry moments he was a part of, my dad wasn't always sold out for Christ. My mom shared how my dad was pretty rowdy when he was in the air force. He was a sergeant during the Vietnam War, stationed in Scotland. He loved all things Scottish, Irish, and English, something he passed on to me.

We used to laugh when my mom showed us pictures of all the girls he hung out with in England. She poked fun at him for dating a girl in London named Monique. He just laughed it off and said, "What can I say? The ladies loved me!" He had a dry and oftentimes irreverent sense of humor—a combo that most people thought was contradictory to ministry but one that was genuine for my dad. I've come to realize that his humor was one of his greatest assets. It made him relatable and accessible to everyone—well, everyone but the stuffy, legalistic Christians. But I think he was okay with that, and honestly, so am I.

My dad's given name was Clyde Albert McBrayer, after my grandfather. Not only was his name just awful, but it also didn't fit his personality. When he was in high school, people started calling him Sonny, probably because of his personality, and the nickname just stuck. He was Sonny McBrayer from then on.

It took me getting into my 40s before I realized that my dad had all these amazing qualities. It was because he recognized these traits in Christ first and then just passed on the gift God had given him.

FIVE:
THE LACK OF LIBERTY

Liberty University is in Lynchburg, Virginia, a little less than 800 miles from where I lived in Riverview, Florida. I left home right after I graduated from high school because I had to rehearse over the summer with the Sounds of Liberty. I have vague memories of packing my stuff and putting everything in the back of my dad's blue Ford Econoline van. The drive to Virginia was supposed to take 11 and a half hours, but my mother had an upset stomach. My father stopped and bought her some Alka-Seltzer, which actually turned out to be Efferdent denture cleaner. Now she *really* had an upset stomach, and after stopping multiple times for her to puke and then a quick stop at the ER, we made it to Lynchburg in about 15 hours.

Since I wasn't allowed to have a car at school my freshman year (such a lame rule), any transportation on and off campus had to be at the mercy of people I had never met before. That did not make me happy.

I have a clear memory of lying on the top bunk in my dorm room after I'd been there about a month, staring up at the ceiling and thinking, *Why doesn't this feel right?* It wasn't because people weren't welcoming because most of them were. They seemed genuinely glad to have me in the Sounds of Liberty, but from the moment I walked on campus, I felt like a square peg in a round hole. I can't explain it except to say that college, particularly a Baptist college, was very different than I had expected. Both of my other brothers had gone off to college, and their experiences weren't anything like mine.

The first night at Liberty after my parents settled me into my dorm room and said goodbye, I started to wonder if I'd be able to handle it. I desperately wanted to call them and tell them to come back and get me. Part of my anxiety was because I was away from home. I had a close relationship with both my parents, and it was difficult knowing I would have to be at school over the summer and then begin classes in the fall. No more trips to the beach. No more summer hangouts with my friends. To make matters worse, because it was such a conservative Baptist university, students had zero—and I mean *zero*—freedom.

During that first summer, it became painfully obvious how different I was from the typical Liberty student. Let me share a situation that will make this point clear. The Sounds of Liberty was traveling, singing at various churches and events all summer. We were on the bus driving back from a gig somewhere in Virginia, and everybody started telling jokes and laughing. Of course, I wanted to be part of it. I just thought we were telling jokes and didn't consider whether or not the jokes were clean or appropriate. So I jumped in and said, "I've got one! I've got one!" and I told my joke.

I can't repeat it here because I don't want to offend anybody, but it wasn't as terrible as you're thinking. It wasn't suggestive or crass, but I guess it was a little bit more adult-oriented. Heck, my father is the one who originally told me the joke, and we both thought it was hilarious (yet another reason why I loved my pop).

Let's just say the silence that followed created an awkward moment. No one laughed—I mean, no one! In fact, I'm fairly certain I could hear crickets chirping somewhere in the distance. Some of the senior members of the group looked at me, silently saying, *How dare you!* I was all but rebuked for it and completely humiliated. I believe that one, slightly questionable joke cemented my character from then on with my group mates. The core group of people I lived and traveled with now viewed me as a maverick or loose cannon.[1]

The Sounds of Liberty was singing in uber-conservative churches, and the group was terrified that I would say something offensive. Fellow singers said, "Jody, just don't say anything" or "You need to know when to just shut up and sing." There was no mistaking how they really felt about me. Some of it was because of the joke. Some of it was because I didn't speak Christianese like most of them. Some of it was because I was a freshman in a group that was mostly juniors and seniors. Now that I think back on it, maybe they were right, but it didn't help me embrace the Christian college experience any faster and only added to my overwhelming desire to go home.

About midway through my freshman year, I called my dad and told him how we had to wear a necktie and dress pants to class every day and how I had to hide my Amy Grant CDs (we weren't allowed to listen to Amy Grant—Amy Grant, for Pete's sake!). However, Sandi Patty and the Gaithers were totally acceptable.

---

1. It's killing me not to share the joke with you, but I can't in this book. If you ever see me in person, remind me, and I will happily tell you.

Basically, if you couldn't operate heavy machinery while listening to it, the music was acceptable by Liberty's standards.

My dad just chuckled on the other end of the line. When I asked him why he was laughing, he said, "Because I knew there would be no liberty at Liberty." He thought it was so funny and probably figured it would be good for my character. I, on the other hand, was not laughing.

I told him I wanted to come home.

"No way! You're not coming home. You need to stay there and stick it out. Be a man; do the work," my dad stated. And so I did— for three years. But I did not like it, and I was not happy.

During my junior year, I got a job working off campus at a restaurant called the Ground Round that had a bar on one side and a restaurant on the other. I made great money waiting tables, but the place was full of smokers. After every shift, I literally smelled like an ashtray. My roommates at the time, Jason and Jeremy Breland (Roger's sons), joked that they would be asleep, and when I opened the door, they would wake up and see something like a giant cigarette butt standing in the doorway. The one good thing about working off campus was that I had permission to stay out past curfew, which was 11:00 p.m. on weekdays and midnight on Fridays and Saturdays.

My coping mechanism for feeling inadequate is typically food, but in college for some reason, it became exercise, specifically running. I began running five to 10 miles every night. After work, I changed out of my smoky clothes, put on my running shoes, and slipped out the nonguarded back entrance of campus. (Yes, you read that correctly. There were guarded entrances. It was like a prison camp, only with worse food.) I ran around the mall and all over town. I ran for hours, like Forrest Gump. It was therapeutic and before long became advantageous to my otherwise portly waistline. When I came to Liberty, I was wearing a 36-inch waist. When I left, I was in size 31. Oh, to be young again.

Sometimes, I just needed to sneak away—disappear. But there were only a few places I could do that. I used to borrow cars from friends and drive to Lynchburg's little municipal airport. I sat in the grass as the sun set, looked up at the sky, and watched the airplanes land and take off. In those moments, I would have given anything to be on one of those airplanes—flying anywhere but where I was. With each passing month, my homesickness wasn't any better. If I'm completely honest with myself, I'll have to admit that I can't put all the blame on Liberty. The more alienated I felt, the more I pushed away any chance of feeling at home there.

There were several difficult moments during my third and final year at Liberty. I reached the point where I couldn't take it anymore. In my heart and mind, I was done. After my junior year, I did not return.

Liberty has changed drastically in the years since I left. It is much more laid-back and accepting than it was 25 years ago. Students can wear shorts and T-shirts to class. That may not sound like a big deal, but I have vivid memories of sitting through an hour and a half theology class while a necktie and sheer boredom choked the life out of me.

I've spent the better part of my adult life feeling like I had a character flaw—that I wasn't a good enough Christian because I told a naughty joke, had a beer with my dinner, or said a curse word when I hit my finger with a hammer.

Higher education establishments usually play a vital role in shaping a person's core beliefs. The tragedy is that I have many friends who left for college with a heart to go into full-time ministry or become a missionary only to return home an agnostic a few semesters later.

Here's a little piece of advice for any young people reading this (or parents of young people). Whatever school you decide to attend, do the work to understand that school's core values before you enroll. You want your values and the school's values to match or at least come close. If you attend a conservative Christian school and act like hell on wheels—you drink, you smoke, you do drugs, you sleep around—and the school administration kicks you out, you can't really blame the school. You went there with full knowledge of their expectations.

On the other hand, maybe you've been sheltered and aren't ready for a secular university where no one is policing what students do with their free time. I went to Liberty because I wanted to eventually sing in TRUTH, and my parents and I didn't stop to think about whether or not I'd be a good fit with Liberty's culture. Maybe that's not entirely true. After all, my dad evidently knew I'd struggle, and it was a lesson I had to learn the hard way.

I wasn't hell on wheels at Liberty—nowhere near that bad. I was actually a pretty good kid while I was there. I just didn't fit the conservative Christian mold and was in conflict with myself the entire time, wondering what was wrong with me.

For the record, I also made some lifelong friendships at Liberty, people I have stayed in contact with to this day. I wouldn't trade that for anything in the world, but the people I'm still friends with were the people who were just like me—square pegs in round holes. We were a group of misfits who weren't really cut out to be fundamental Baptist Christian kids, and we were branded as such.

* * *

There were several positive things at Liberty, and one of them was my amazing voice teacher. His name was Dr. Hugo, and I was his student for nearly two years. He was a traditionalist when it came to voice and instruction, much like my first teacher, Eugenia Halston.

When we first started working together, he was staunch and unwavering about teaching me classical voice. That meant using only proper technique and singing only classical music—in laymen's terms, an opera singer.

Dr. Hugo knew I wasn't a classical singer; everybody knew I wanted to sing pop music. But he was determined that if I was going to be under his tutelage, I was going to learn the classics and classical technique first.

For the first year, I did what he told me to do, albeit with a bit of frustration. I have to admit that now I'm very glad I did because he taught me techniques I still implement today before and during every concert. He taught me what it means to preserve your voice, that it's okay to use your head voice to hit some of the high notes, that not everything has to be sung in full voice. He said that if I was going to sing high, I could use a controlled head voice to stay high, and I didn't have to push my voice so high that I could risk damaging it. He taught me the importance of proper posture and voice placement. I have no doubt his lessons are largely responsible for why I'm still singing.

The first year I sang with Dr. Hugo, he had me sing in German and occasionally Italian. He was teaching me about breath support and control, as well as chipping away at my bad vocal habits. That's how I found the first layers of my voice and the beginning of being comfortable having such a high voice. Before that, I often covered my voice and tried to sing like Michael McDonald because I was insecure about how I sounded. Dr. Hugo helped me understand that I had a higher tessitura, or vocal placement, and should be comfortable with that. My job was to learn how to control it.

I credit him with being the first person to peel back the layers of my voice and help me understand that I can't go from nothing to a hundred and sing as hard as I want. He was also the first person to teach me what it meant to be a good steward of my voice and the gift God gave me.

As time passed, we nurtured a relationship and became friends. Recently, I visited the school, and he was still teaching. I hugged his neck and told him how much I appreciated him and the lasting impression he had made on me. I think he was surprised that I remembered, but I did, and I always will.

In my second year of vocal instruction, I had to tell Dr. Hugo that my desire wasn't to sing classical music. "Listen, I love what you're teaching me, but this is not the kind of music I'm going to sing for the rest of my life. I'm called to be a pop singer, and I need you to help me navigate pop music."

Pop music wasn't something he did *at all*. In fact, he often commented negatively on how horrible pop CCM artists' techniques were. But he was kind and chose to help me anyway. For recitals, I had to sing something classical, but he helped me sing some of my ensemble music during my voice lessons and helped me translate to contemporary what he had taught me classically.

I don't know this for certain, but I have a feeling that the reason Dr. Hugo is still teaching (and he probably would hate to admit it) is because he knows deep down how important it is to instill in young people the idea of preservation and stamina, regardless of the genre they're singing.

Today, Liberty employs professors who help students with pop voices and pop singing. At the time of the writing of this book, Mindy Damon is working with these voices, and I'm so glad she is. Most of the singers who major in vocal performance aren't going to sing classical and opera; they're going to sing worship, pop, and rock music.

If these vocal students aren't taught how to preserve their voices—their instrument—they're not going to last five years on the road. The schedule, the music, and often the audio can be brutal. By audio, I mean not every performance setting allows for in-ear monitors or excellent acoustics, and often singers oversing when the circumstances aren't adequate. Vocal performers need to know the proper skills so they can survive a career as a full-time musician, whatever genre they choose to pursue.

While I had the benefit of learning voice under Dr. Hugo, I continued to struggle to find my place at school (I know, I know, not this again). Between what was happening with my dad at my home church and my time at Liberty, I'd be lying if I didn't say my faith was affected. I learned a lot about the kind of Christian I *didn't* want to be. I don't want to generalize because there were and still are some wonderful, loving people at Liberty. But as I've already said, when you're already feeling insecure and inadequate, the judgmental folks tend to stand out as a glaring example of the majority.

People like Dr. David Randlett were the exception. He was the head of the Fine Arts Department, and his son Paul was in Sounds of Liberty with me and also a close friend. Dr. Randlett and his wife, MJ, opened their home to me as an escape, and I often crashed in their basement just to get away from campus when I was having a difficult time. The whole family was kind and caring, and I owe a lot to them for helping me navigate that season of my life when I felt so lost.

As I look back on those times, it's obvious now that those tumultuous phases were likely early signs of depression. I remember the feelings of darkness and loneliness that I couldn't control, but I was too young to recognize them as anything other than raw emotions. It was 1991, and few people talked about depression back then.

Another positive part of my last year at Liberty was being roommates with Jason and Jeremy Breland, the sons of TRUTH founder and director, Roger Breland. It wasn't planned; it just fell into place after Jason and I ended up in a production together. I believe that was the catalyst for how I would transition out of Liberty and begin traveling with TRUTH.

Jason was involved in music as well and part of another ensemble on campus called Light. Their music was more pop, more contemporary, and a little more edgy than the Sounds of Liberty, which was more conservative since we sang on *The Old Time Gospel Hour* television broadcast every weekend with Dr. Jerry Falwell.

One night Jason and I were hanging out in our dorm room— Jason on the bottom bunk and me on the top. Jason said, partly joking and partly serious, "Jody, you should come over and sing with Light. It's more your style." It started to become a running joke in our dorm room, and we mentioned it often.

Jason and Jeremy both knew I couldn't leave Sounds since I'd lose my scholarship. They just loved giving me a hard time. That wasn't the only thing they made fun of me for. I could be a little heavy-handed with the cologne back then, and when I got up early for class when Jeremy and Jason were still sleeping, they noticed my use of cologne. They often teased me later in the day, claiming I had doused myself with 20 sprays of cologne that morning. I swore they were crazy, but they were probably close. It was ridiculous. Twenty sprays? I must have smelled awful. I am so grateful for their friendship during that last year at Liberty. They were hilarious, and there was a lot of laughter that helped me get through it, even if it was at my own expense.

TRUTH came to Liberty several times to perform, and one of those times, I decided to audition. When I introduced myself to Roger Breland again, surprisingly, he remembered me from the Carpenter's Home Church concert. He remembered my father charging the stage and tugging on his pant leg. He also knew I was roommates with his sons and said, "You're a great singer, and I think you could have a place in TRUTH, but you really must finish school first."

So I focused on working through the remainder of my time at Liberty. At this point, my grades were not great. I struggled to stay focused in class, but my time there wasn't all unproductive. In fact, I think I learned some valuable lessons in humility and life. Scholastically, I didn't learn much, but the life experience was priceless. My dad used to tell me, "Humble yourself before the Lord because if you don't, He will humble you, and when He humbles you, it hurts." Growing up, I never understood what he meant. But I was about to get my first real lesson.

In spite of my mediocre academic accomplishments, I felt pretty confident in my ability to sing. I figured that I was awarded a scholarship because I'm a good singer. I'm in the Sounds of Liberty, which was considered Liberty's premier group at the time. Subconsciously, I thought pretty highly of myself, which is always a recipe for disaster. Let me tell you about one of my first lessons in humility.

We had chapel on Mondays, Wednesdays, and Fridays. We met in the old gymnasium (that was before they built the Six-Flags-over-Jesus setup they have now). In the old gym, some of the best speakers and musicians came and entered the lives of the students. One of the campus ensemble groups often sang in chapel before the guest speaker got up. On one occasion, a male student was asked to sing a solo before the guest pastor spoke.

I really don't know what my problem was that day. I suppose I was feeling insecure, because the truth is, the guy had a really good voice. But for whatever reason, I was whispering to the person next to me and making fun of him to some of my friends while he sang.

I didn't realize that the dean of students, Vernon Brewer, was sitting behind me. I guess he watched and listened to my stupidity unfold until he'd had enough. He leaned forward and, in front of everybody, said, "You know, it takes a lot of courage to get up there. I think you know that firsthand. Would you want somebody talking about you like this while you were onstage singing? Why don't you show the guy some respect?"

I was stunned, first because I didn't realize Vernon was sitting behind me and second because it made me stop and think, *Oh my gosh, what am I doing?* The guy up there singing was effeminate. He was a high tenor. He was all I was insecure about, and I was making fun of him. I was doing the exact thing I hated other people to do to me.

Vernon Brewer was right; I was being a jerk. I apologized to the dean and to the guy I had made fun of, and he didn't even know what I'd done. The funny thing is, I eventually ended up becoming friends with the guy and grew to respect him. Isn't that how it usually goes? The person doing the bullying is lashing out from a place of jealousy or pain. Looking back on it now, I feel so stupid. I'll always be grateful that Vernon Brewer kicked my butt a little because, apparently, I needed it.

Roger (or, as we all called him, B or JRB) came to Liberty to visit his sons toward the end of my junior year. He and I had talked a bit about how I might want to leave school and come on the road. I told him again that I wanted to audition. He reluctantly agreed, but first, he asked me to hop in his car so we could take a ride.

We drove around the Liberty University campus, which didn't take very long because it was about half the size it is today, and he said to me in his southern, authoritative drawl, "Jody, I need a tenor, and I know you're unhappy here. If you really think this is what you want to do, then I'm going to give you a chance. Just don't disappoint me."

He said a lot more in the car that day—stipulations, conditions, understandings. The one thing I was sure of by the time he dropped me back at my dorm was that when I was done with this semester, I was joining Roger Breland on the road with TRUTH. That was the start of my journey to becoming a professional musician. For the first time in a very long time, I was happy.

I was just 17 credits shy of getting my degree, and while that stings a little sometimes, I know how I felt when I was at Liberty. It wasn't where I was supposed to be. Hindsight being 20/20, I should have finished my degree, and if my daughter were in the same position, I would tell her to finish. But alas, that's the ignorance of youth.

My dad knew I was miserable. When I came home during Christmas breaks, I never wanted to go back when the break ended. No parent wants to see their kid go through that. That summer, I finally said, "Dad, I'm not going back. I spoke to Mr. Breland, and he wants me to come and sing with TRUTH. I think that's what I'm going to do."

My dad knew it was time, and he gave me his blessing. Interestingly, after I'd been with TRUTH for a month or two, my dad called and told me that my final grades from my junior year had come in the mail. When I asked him how they were, he responded, "Well, let's just put it this way, son. College isn't for everybody."

Liberty University has become a world-renowned Christian university. It is no longer the school it was when I was there. The students and faculty are diverse and welcoming. The educational opportunities are vast and practically unlimited. When I was a student there, I believe both the school and I were struggling to find our identities. I've had the tremendous honor to return several times as both a guest performer and an instructor. I even hope my daughter will consider attending Liberty University when it comes time for her to go to college.

And no, this wasn't a paid endorsement.

SIX:
THE ROAD

TRUTH—an acronym that stands for Trust, Receive, Unchangeable, True Happiness [in Jesus]—was a traveling music group founded in 1971 by Roger Breland and based in Mobile, Alabama. For more than 30 years, TRUTH traveled the United States and all over the world, recorded nearly 50 studio albums, and had hundreds of members, many who have gone on to be successful artists and musicians. In 2000, TRUTH and Roger Breland were inducted into the Gospel Music Hall of Fame, a moment and honor that was unquestionably earned and well-deserved.

Somehow, B always found amazing singers. They were like a moth to his flame. He now sponsors groups at the University of Mobile where, at the time of this publication, he is the executive director of the Roger Breland Center for the Performing Arts, as well as dean emeritus of the Alabama School of the Arts. I still shake my head at the amount of excellent talent he has surrounded himself with.

Walking onto that TRUTH bus for the first time, I had obvious expectations, and needless to say, the first couple of weeks were eye-opening. First, the pay was awful. In fact, it was so awful that it's notorious. I made $30 every two weeks and $2.50 a day for lunch.

When I first started with them in the early '90s, we stopped for lunch every day at fast-food choices near an interstate exit or at a mall. The road manager walked down the aisle of the bus passing out $5 bills. He said as he handed each person the money, "Today and tomorrow. Today and tomorrow. Today and tomorrow." That meant half of that money was for lunch today, and the other half was for lunch tomorrow. I kid you not.

Even in 1992, you couldn't go into a Taco Bell and eat much on $2.50. But I settled into the fact that this was just life on the road, and I was so happy to be there that I didn't care. And I actually lost a little weight. We stayed in hotel rooms on our days off, but on normal days—concert days—we stayed with host families. Typically, they were people who attended the church where we'd be singing that night. Most of the time, these families were kind and generous with simple but adequate lodging. However, that wasn't always the case.

The *other* host homes should have never considered being a host home to begin with. My most memorable host-home experience was in Arkansas. We arrived late one night after a concert and pulled into the driveway. There were no lights on anywhere outside or inside the house. It was dark, I mean Darth Vader dark. There was barely enough light to make out the full-sized washer and dryer in the front yard that had been made into a planter—recycling at its best.

When we got inside the house, the host walked me down the hall to my room, which was also pitch-black. She apologized and said she was having trouble with her electricity and that we wouldn't be able to turn on the lights in the bedroom or the attached bathroom. While I was completely freaked out, I tried to be kind and told her it was no problem.

As I was getting ready for bed, my eyes somewhat adjusted to the low light, and I made my way into the adjoining bathroom to brush my teeth. I could see the white marble sink to the left and the white marble tub to the right. I felt for the faucet, turned on the water, brushed my teeth and went back to the bedroom to sleep.

The next morning, I awoke to a room filled with sunlight. I got up and gathered my toiletries to take a shower. When I went to the bathroom and pulled the shower curtain back, I noticed that the veins of colored marble running through the white tub were actually lines of ants—hundreds and hundreds of black ants covered the entire tub, making a line across the bathroom floor and up the wall to the sink where they almost completely covered the surface.

I had left my toothbrush sitting on the edge of the sink, and it, too, was now overrun by ants. I quickly gathered my things, minus the toothbrush (obviously), got dressed, and announced that I was ready to leave. Someone in the group gave me a new toothbrush, and I washed up as best I could that morning in the restroom on the bus.

Being on the road full-time was an interesting experiment in life. Up to that point, I hadn't had a serious romantic relationship. I was far too immature to be part of that. I had dated a couple girls in college, and one of them I had liked very much. She was a wonderful girl, but the relationship ended rather abruptly when I left to go on the road. I never considered how difficult that must have been for her, but I was focused on fulfilling my dream.

When I joined TRUTH, it was like taking a crash course in life, music, being on the road, and relationships all at once. You learn a lot about people whether you want to or not. I didn't really have a choice—we were crammed into a bus like sardines, and as you can imagine, it gets interesting when you trap 16 people in a 45-foot-long, 8-foot-wide traveling house.

There were rules, strictly enforced rules that every new TRUTH member was handed when they first walked on the bus. They were affectionately called the Trules and were written by people who had spent way too much time on the road. There were rules like "Don't slam the doors! Someone is always trying to sleep" and "The 'toy' (bus toilet) is for going number one only. Never, under any circumstance, are you to do a number two in the toy." This is actually common bus etiquette on every motor coach and tour bus, but at the time, I had no idea.

Other Trules were things like "Don't let the sink water run for too long; we aren't hooked up to Niagara Falls" and "If somebody's name is on it, it belongs to them. Don't touch without asking." And there were rules like "No popcorn in the microwave. It stinks up the bus, and the smell wakes people up because, again, someone is always sleeping." At the time, I found it all a bit silly, but I was new and did my best to follow every rule. Only after being on the bus for an extended period of time did the rules start to make more sense. However, I remember initially reading the list of Trules and thinking, *What have I gotten myself into?*

One funny story about those first days, weeks, and months on the road involved one of the authors of the so-called Trules, Mike Childers. He was the road manager and drummer for the group, and his younger brother, Mark, played bass. Some of the people on the bus, including the Childers brothers, had been on the road for five or six years at that point, and they were simply exhausted.

Mike, who would eventually become the drummer for Avalon, had been on the road a long time, and you could tell in his countenance that he was, well, done. He had gotten married, and he and his wife were both on the road as newlyweds trying to make it work. I'm pretty sure life wasn't going all that well for them.

Early one morning, Mike was sitting in the driver's seat of the bus (did I mention he also drove the bus occasionally?) waiting for the hosts to drop everyone off. I was one of the last ones to walk up the bus steps that morning, and just being happy to be there, I was singing at the top of my lungs. I don't remember what I was singing, but I do remember that Mike grabbed my arm as I walked by him, looked me in the eyes, and said—with a look like he wanted to kill me—"You know what? You don't have to sing every time you walk on this bus!"

I was just a kid of 21 and excited to be on the bus, but his outburst and the way he said it did take a little wind out of my sails. Mike was formidable and intimidating, and I was terrified of him. That moment cemented my fear of him, and I gave him a wide berth for the remainder of his time in the group. I was careful never to sing in front of Mike again unless it was on the stage. I don't recall us ever speaking again, and he ended up leaving the group a few months later. Mike and his brother, Mark, went on to be part of Avalon's band, and we later laughed about that moment and many more as we relived stories of being on the TRUTH bus.

My transition from Liberty to TRUTH was fast. I left Liberty and flew to Orlando where I immediately started rehearsals with Leigh (Darby) Cappillino (currently in Point of Grace), Karen Fairchild (now a member of the country group Little Big Town), Russ Lee (now in NewSong), and several other new singers. Alicia Williamson was the vocal director at the time and a well-known TRUTH member.

She walked us through each song and taught us what parts to sing, the necessary choreography, and what it took to recreate the signature TRUTH sound—something that was called singing on the breath. I'm still not sure where that expression came from, but it did describe that unique sound that TRUTH had. There was a vocal cohesion and execution that was, and still is, unlike any other vocal group I have ever heard. I learned all of that in a Motel 6 double hotel room near Lake Buena Vista in Orlando, Florida.

TRUTH was preparing to record a new album when I joined the group. It was to be my first legitimate experience in the studio as a recording artist. The record was called *More Than You'll Ever Imagine*, and somehow, I ended up with two solo leads for "Power of Praise" and "So Far, So Good." I never once questioned whether or not I had the talent to run in that crowd; I just thought I was the coolest.

We went back to Orlando a few weeks later to record, and I met our producer, Don Koch, for the first time. Don and long-time TRUTH producer Steven V. Taylor were sharing production responsibilities. Don is an accomplished songwriter and producer and well-known in the industry. Steven was a TRUTH alum and an accomplished arranger and producer in his own right. He had produced many TRUTH records, and having him on board was a given. We went into the studio, and "So Far, So Good" was first on the recording schedule. It also happened to be co-written by Don Koch himself. No pressure!

I don't remember what my frame of mind was that day as I stepped into the studio, but I do remember it was early in the morning, and I was nervous and feeling insecure and intimidated by the process and the people. I'd done a couple recordings in college with the Sounds of Liberty, but I'd never been in a recording studio—nothing like this.

I walked in and noticed the scent of cedar from the wooden planks covering the walls. Steven and Don were both there that morning doing the producer thing, encouraging me, telling me I was going to sound great on the song. There was also a well-known studio technician working the helm who shall remain nameless. He didn't have much to say to me, but then again, that wasn't his role. His job was to push buttons and splice reels. Back then, digital recording hadn't happened yet, so everything was still recorded on tape. When a song had to be edited, someone actually had to slice the tape and then put it back together. It seems so archaic now, but millions of recordings were done this way. In fact, some of the most iconic music ever recorded was done on tape.

Once the microphone was situated and the levels right, I started to sing. I kept struggling to get the lyrics right. Obviously, my anxiety wasn't helping. I messed up on the same spot over and over, which is common with people in the studio, but I didn't have the experience to understand that. At one point, I stopped singing because I was growing frustrated, and the technician pushed the talk-back button and said, "Hey, let's try that again, okay?" to which I replied, "Sure. I'm sorry. There goes my professional music career." And I just laughed. I guess the technician didn't realize the talk-back button was still pushed down or stuck, and he chuckled sarcastically and said to Steven and Don, "Well, I don't think we really have to worry about that, do we?" They all laughed and made more snarky comments.

Ouch!

To add insult to injury, later that week there was a moment when the entire group was in the studio singing together, and Don specifically singled out my voice and asked me to step out of the room, that it wasn't working. No explanations. No apologies. Just "Get out."

Shattered!

Fast-forward a couple decades. In 2020, Don Koch produced Avalon's record *Called*. I consider him a friend and have nothing but respect for him and all he has accomplished in this industry. We have spoken about this situation, and while I'm not sure he remembers it, he does remember giving me other nuggets of advice such as how I should leave the studio because he didn't think I could sing. It felt like he was telling me, "Well, Jody, welcome to the next level. Here is where you finally find out you just don't have what it takes to make it."

All those words cut deeply. They stayed with me for a long time. In fact, it wasn't until two records in with Avalon—when we started working with Brown Bannister—that Brown was able to help me get to the root of my studio insecurity. Both the studio engineer and Don's words had planted a seed. I started believing something that wasn't true, and to this day, when I am in the studio working with Don, those insecurities creep back in. I start believing the lie once more. Just to be completely candid, I still don't think Don really cares for my voice, and if it were anyone else, I wouldn't care. When it's your producer, that's a completely different story.

After that initial experience with TRUTH in the studio, I started overcompensating—doing whatever I could to change my voice so it would be more likable, more professionally acceptable. I began covering my voice, darkening my tone to try to make it sound more mature, more like a man. I became ultra-sensitive and insecure about my high-pitched tone. I thought the tenor of my voice was the reason no one liked to hear me in the studio. It wasn't until Brown took the time to knock some sense into me that I began to accept the gift that God had given me the way it was naturally intended.

I still look back on some of those old TRUTH videos (many are on YouTube or shared on Facebook), and I think how clueless that kid singing onstage was. I thought I was ready to be out there. I was desperate to leave college and pursue my dream. But it wasn't long before the life I had chosen started to close in on me. Life on the road wasn't what I thought it would be. It wasn't glamorous or profitable, and, unlike when I was a kid in the little town of Riverview, not everyone liked the way I sang.

My perceptions of life on the road quickly faded as weeks turned to months and months to years. When people, especially artsy, creative, passionate, emotional musicians, are crammed on a bus with almost no personal space, it's a recipe for dysfunction. Inevitably, people start dating, pairing off, and hooking up. I wasn't immune to that; I had my share of relationships too.

Two couples I traveled with got engaged and then married while we were on the road. I was with one of the guys when he was shopping for the engagement ring. He was so sure, so convinced, and seemed so ready. I knew the girl was not. Several of the other guys tried to talk to him about it, but he wouldn't hear them. The day after he proposed, his fiancée came on the bus with some of the other singers, myself included, and while her fiancé was off the bus, she said, "Well, I said yes. I did what you guys wanted." *Wait! What* we *wanted?* I remember thinking, *This is not a good sign.*

They asked many of us to sing and be part of their wedding, and we all did. I believe they tried hard to make it work for a while, but it just wasn't meant to be from the start, and I think they both knew it. They divorced several years later. The other couple is still happily married.

When I sang at the first couple's wedding, I recall wondering what was going through both of their hearts and heads as they stood looking at each other. Did they have doubts then? Neither of them seemed very happy to be there. Was it the pressure of being crammed on a bus together 24/7?

No one but the two of them will ever know for sure. They are both now remarried to other people and very happy. They've both had strong careers in country music and have accomplished great things apart from one another. I still see her occasionally and speak to her more than I do him, but from my perspective, nothing is wasted, and whatever time they spent together, God meant it for a reason and hopefully they learned and grew from it.

When you're on a bus 260 days out of the year—and I don't mean any disrespect or offense—everybody looks good. We were all in our 20s and in the prime of our lives. Hormones being what they are, I'm not going to pretend that it was like riding the Partridge Family bus. It wasn't a convent, and no one took an oath of celibacy. There were questionable decisions being made all the time, and JRB did his best to keep situations at bay.

This sexual tension was obvious when TRUTH was going to purchase a new bus. Everyone wanted a bus with a shower because it would make life on the road much easier (like when your host home is infested with ants and you can't shower). When pushed one day about the subject, JRB seemed tired of being asked, so he responded, "Y'all wanna know why I won't get a bus with a shower?" Everyone stared at him, waiting for a logical reason. He said, "Cuz y'all will just get in there and get naked." Everyone laughed. I mean, obviously, that's what you do in a shower, but the subtext was not lost on anyone, and we dropped the case for a new bus with a shower.

I know everyone would like to believe that because it was a Christian bus on a Christian tour and everybody there was 100 percent sold out for Jesus that nothing ever happened apart from fasting and prayer. For the most part, everyone's heart was in the right place, but when you put a group of human beings together, they all make poor decisions at times.

I was naïve when I joined TRUTH. Even though I'd been through most of college, Liberty was far from being a typical college experience. I'm sure things were going on there that I didn't realize, but you never saw it. People were adamant about hiding their less-than-perfect behavior and then pretending they were above reproach. Obviously, I know now that no one is above reproach, and at times, everybody is a mess. But living on that bus with 16 other people, I wasn't prepared to see the best and worst of them. And some of the worst of them brought out the worst in me. It's nobody's fault; it's just part of growing up.

I was a grown man then, even though I was only in my early 20s, and I didn't know whether to "scratch my watch or wind my butt" (*Steel Magnolias* reference). I didn't know the first thing about life, and yet there I was thinking I was prepared to live it. It wasn't until I got out there and people in their mid-30s who had way more experience at life and the real world said to me, "This is just how things are done. You scratch my back, I'll scratch yours" that I understood how they worked.

If you fall in line with those people instead of who you know you really are, you will make decisions that are contrary to who you want to be—who God wants you to be. It's the age-old story, but it was being played out by an amateur, and I wasn't prepared to navigate it properly.

Expectations have always been difficult for me, maybe because I'm usually oblivious to them until I fall short of the expectations someone has of me. When I realize it, it destroys me, usually because I've disappointed someone. It was during this time on the TRUTH bus that I came face-to-face with how short my shortcomings could be. I was forced to.

At 23, there was a lot I hadn't done. Being in TRUTH made me feel like the cord had finally been cut from home. I felt like I was on my first job, an adult in the world. But I was also realizing that the longer I stayed on the road, the less I was being a good steward of that opportunity.

In high school, I was a pretty good kid. I barely drank and was always the designated driver. Being a rebel just wasn't who I was. So when I finally came face-to-face with the fact that I wasn't as perfect as I thought I was and that within me was the ability to make a mistake and also disappoint people I cared about, it was a hard pill to swallow. It was especially hard because my parents had so much faith in me. It's tough when somebody believes in you, loves you, and views you as nearly perfect, and then you have to tell them, "Hey, I'm not everything you think I am."

Now that I'm a dad, there's a difference between what a parent sees as a big deal and what a child sees as a big deal. I know I'm never going to change how I feel about my daughter. She could come to me tomorrow and say, "Dad, I've committed a horrible crime," and I would tell her, "You have to go to jail. You have to pay the price for your crime, but it doesn't change the fact that I love you." I may be heartbroken, in disbelief that my daughter was capable of something so awful, but it wouldn't change how much I love her.

I think that's how Christ sees us. His love for us doesn't change, no matter how much we disappoint Him. Adam and Eve ate the forbidden fruit. God told them not to do that, and they did it anyway, but then they realized they were naked and tried to cover up. They had to pay the consequences for their sin.

We all pay the consequences for the wrongs we do. We live in a world that loves to think there aren't any consequences and that we can live however we want. But I think we all know deep down that's just not the case. I don't think God is sitting up there waiting to get us back for everything we do wrong; I believe His love is unconditional and His forgiveness is endless. But God did say, "Be not deceived; God is not mocked: for whatsoever a man soweth, that shall he also reap" (Gal. 6:7 KJV).

In TRUTH, it was common for people to come and go. We had a revolving door of singers. That's just how it was, and you mostly got used to it. In March 1993, I had been on the road nearly two years with TRUTH, and it was my time to leave.

The closing of this chapter of my life was the result of a poor decision I made. I won't go into any detail about it because it would hurt people, and that is not the purpose of this book. Its purpose is to show that even in this difficult moment when I failed miserably, God was in it. He was working even though I felt like a complete and utter failure.

Roger found out what I had done and called me in for a meeting one night. It was not a pleasant conversation. He was gracious. I knew he was hurt and frustrated, but he never raised his voice or said anything mean, and it was clear that I had disappointed him. As he talked to me, I remembered the conversation we'd had in the car at Liberty two years earlier before he brought me into the group—"Don't disappoint me."

It was difficult for both of us. I must give Roger proper credit; he didn't fire me, although he sure should have. He was kind, gracious, and truly concerned about my well-being. He always treated me with respect. He treated me like a father would his son. Even though he was upset, he asked me to stay. He believed in me, and that is something I will never, ever forget. I saw Christ in him.

At that point, I planned to stay, but God had a different plan, and my time with TRUTH was about to come to an end.

SEVEN:
THE PRODIGAL

We had a day off—something that didn't happen very often in TRUTH. It was just two days after JRB had pulled me aside and confronted me about what I had done. I was still wincing from it, feeling out of place and overwhelmed. In my heart, I knew I had to call home and talk to my parents about it, but I was terrified to do so. They would be so disappointed in me.

This particular day off involved waterskiing at a cabin on a lake provided by a generous host. I sat on the dock and watched everyone having an amazing time, and my heart was broken. I couldn't get past what I had done, and the guilt was eating at me. Because I'm someone who prefers to rip off the Band-Aid rather than peel it off slowly, I decided to walk into the house and call home. I didn't want to tell my parents, and I didn't have to, but I needed to talk to someone about it and felt like it was the best thing to do.

They were both excited to hear from me. My father answered and told my mother to pick up on the bedroom line. After the usual pleasantries, I told them there was something they needed to know. I began telling them the entire story, ending with how JRB had pulled me aside a couple nights ago and confronted me. For what seemed like forever, there was silence on the other end of the line.

My mother finally spoke and asked a couple questions, but my father didn't speak, which was completely out of character for him. It was in that silence that I created a scenario of deep frustration, shame, and disappointment. Finally, my father said, "I want you to come home. What city are you in?" I told him that I hadn't been fired and that I didn't think I could leave. He was insistent, so I told him what city we were in. He said, "I will purchase a ticket, and you can pick it up at the airport. Have someone take you there first thing in the morning." I agreed, and we hung up. My heart caved. I had let him down, and it was almost too much for me to bear.

I was sharing a host home with Jason Breland, and even though we were close, I didn't feel like I could explain to him all the reasons I needed to leave. So I didn't tell him or anyone else I was leaving. After Jason went to bed, I asked our host if he would mind taking me to the airport early the next morning. I also asked him to please not say anything to anyone until after I was gone.

He was a very kind man and didn't ask any questions. The next morning, he woke me before the sun was up. He had made breakfast for me, but I just pushed the plate around. Then he drove me to the airport. When we arrived, he walked around to let me out of the car, handed me my suitcase, and said, "I don't know what's going on, and it's none of my business, but I will be praying for you. I hope it all works out." He shook my hand, and I thanked him. Then I watched him get back in the car and drive away.

I stood on the curb and began to cry. I didn't know if I could go home and face my father. I had no idea what to expect and could barely make myself walk into the small, regional airport. I made my way in as the sun began coming up on the horizon. I walked up to the empty Delta Airlines counter where a young girl had just come on duty. I told her I was picking up a ticket, gave her my name, and showed her my ID.

She printed the ticket for me, checked my baggage, and gave me the boarding pass. She said, "Mr. McBrayer, you're in seat 1A, first class. You'll board in 20 minutes through the gate to your left."

I stopped. "How did I get in first class? I'm pretty sure that's a mistake."

She smiled. "No, sir. Whoever purchased your ticket purchased a first-class fare. Have a safe trip."

I still thought she was mistaken, but I walked through the metal detector, went to the gate, and boarded my flight home. I stared out the window the entire time, ignoring everyone around me. The pit in my stomach weighed so heavily on me that I could hardly breathe. I now had nowhere to go, no money, no job, and no idea what I was supposed to do next.

I had to connect with another flight in Atlanta. Making my way through the airport, I passed by the gates of flights that were going to Nassau, the Bahamas, and Paris and wished so desperately that I could escape—run away and disappear someplace where no one knew me. As I made my way to the Tampa gate, passengers were already boarding, so I had no time to change my mind. I boarded the plane, took my seat, and stared out the window, wishing the ache in the pit of my stomach would stop.

When I finally landed in Tampa, I took a deep breath and unbuckled my seat belt. This was before September 11, and everyone—passengers and guests—could freely walk to the gate.

Because I was seated in the front, I was the second person off the plane. As I looked down the bridge, I wondered if my father would be there to meet me.

I walked so slowly to the gate that people were pushing past me. As I rounded the corner, I saw my dad standing at the end with tears in his eyes. I began to sob. Of all the gifts my father was blessed with, arguably his greatest was the ability to hug in such a way that made you feel safe, welcome, and okay.

He grabbed me and pulled me close, hugging me for a long time. Then he pulled back, grabbed my chin, and looked me straight in the eye. "No matter where you go, no matter what you do, you can always come home, and I will always love you. Do you understand?" I nodded and sobbed out the words, "I'm so sorry . . ."

Safe. Forgiven. Home. My father was a reflection of our heavenly Father. That's why the story of the prodigal son (Luke 15:11–32) has always meant so much to me. More times than I care to admit, I have been that prodigal son.

The next couple of weeks were challenging. I had moments when I thought, *I'm okay,* and moments when I wasn't too sure. My dad was very patient and loving with me. I'm sure he was disappointed, but he never let it show. We had a couple of hours of conversation when I first came home, and then he and my mother never spoke of it again, at least not with me.

After leaving TRUTH, I had no idea what I would do next. I had so many questions about who I was and what I was meant to do. I took a few weeks to gather myself, spend some time with my family, and detox from road life.

In about my third week home, I got a call from my friend Matthew Cork. He entered TRUTH as a trumpet player at the same time I joined the group, and we became great friends. He left TRUTH shortly before I did to take a job as a part-time worship pastor at a church in California. He also played trumpet part-time at Disneyland. He told me he knew someone who worked for Disneyland who could give me a job if I was interested. It meant I would have to move to California. Well, I didn't have anything else to do, so I said, "Why not?"

I had stayed with a wonderful host family—Gerald and Debbie Barnes—in Southern California when TRUTH passed through there several months earlier, and they told me if I ever needed to, I could come and stay with them for a while to get on my feet. They had heard I was planning on moving to Southern California. They attended the church where Matthew was the worship pastor, and they offered me a place to stay. I took them up on their offer.

I grew very close to them and their three children—Meri, Matt, and Megan. They made me feel at home when I was so far away from anything familiar, and Gerald and Debbie became like second parents to me. They were a refuge in a difficult and wandering time of my life. Their family quickly became my family, and I settled into my new life in California.

Gerald had never been a fan of my traveling with TRUTH because he saw us working so hard and getting paid so little. He was a fair and honest businessman who understood the value of hard work and had become very successful in his own right. He was kind enough to give me a little money and even a car to use. I can't tell you where I would be if they hadn't been so kind to me. I owe a great deal to them that I will never be able to repay. Our lives have changed, many years and miles separate us now, and their kids are grown and have children of their own, but I still consider them like family and miss them greatly.

After I moved to California, the job at Disneyland didn't happen quite as planned. I did a few special event jobs there but had difficulty finding something full-time. Basically, I was unemployed.

Gerald knew I was looking for a job and said to me one day, "Why don't you come and work for me?" He ran an apparel manufacturing company, something I had no clue about, but I liked the idea of working there. I knew Gerald's company was very successful, so on my first day, I wore a nice shirt, dress pants, and expensive shoes.

Gerald met me at the door and walked me out to the warehouse where I met the warehouse manager, who said to me, "Have you ever driven a forklift?" I chuckled and told him I hadn't. "Well, I need you to figure it out and move those boxes onto these pallets."

I looked up at a stack of boxes that went as far as the eye could see in either direction. Here I was, dressed in designer clothes and expecting to be in the executive offices. Instead, I was in the warehouse being told to drive a forklift. I worked that day in my dress clothes and learned how to drive a forklift, but my pride got the best of me. I didn't go the next day and made some stupid excuse about another job interview.

I found out later that Gerald was going to let me work in the warehouse a couple of days, see what I was made of, and then allow me to move into the office. When he told me that, all the blood seemed to drain from my face. I was humiliated and embarrassed that I'd disappointed him. I hate to admit it, but part of me thought I was above working in a warehouse driving a forklift. For all my faults, pride has never been something I've struggled with, but in this instance, I let it get the best of me, and I was mortified.

I eventually ended up taking a full-time job at a luxury retailer. I made okay money and ended up moving out of the Barneses' home and into an apartment with Matthew and another roommate.

I will forever be grateful to Gerald for giving me the chance to work for him. He has never held that experience and my ridiculous behavior over my head. He never judged me. I think he just saw it as a character flaw, which hurts deeper than anything else. People often ask me in interviews or conversations if I have any regrets in my life. Although I've learned not to regret anything because it's all part of my story and what has made me who I am, I would have to say my deepest regret is not returning to work the next day at Gerald's warehouse.

Eventually, I took a job as a part-time music assistant at what was then Yorba Linda Friends Church. It was the same church the Barnes family attended and where Matthew Cork was worship pastor. While I wasn't much of an assistant, probably more of a hired soloist, I loved working at the church and made amazing friendships with many people there. I was also able to start traveling a little again with a small group called BASIX.

Matthew started a group that was similar to TRUTH stylistically but mainly had dates in and around Southern California. While we only traveled occasionally, we had an incredible time together, and I made some hilarious and unforgettable memories with some really cool people.

A year or so after I started working at the church, Matthew and I, along with several of our friends from BASIX and the church staff, decided to take a cruise. When we returned from the cruise, I was surprised to hear that while I was away Bill Gaither had called the Barnes house looking for me. Debbie Barnes passed along his number, and I phoned Bill the minute I got the chance.

He said my name was recommended to him by several people and that he was looking for a tenor to replace Michael English in the Gaither Vocal Band. He asked if I would be interested in flying to Anderson, Indiana, to audition and meet with him. I agreed, playing it cool over the phone. However, the minute I hung up, I had one of those *"Holy crap, I just spoke to Bill Gaither!"* moments. I knew this was going to be my opportunity to get back into the industry again.

Five days later, I flew to Anderson to meet with Bill Gaither. He put me in the studio right away and had me record a couple of songs in which Michael English had carried the lead part. I struggled the entire time. I couldn't hit the notes; I couldn't control my tone or pitch. Something was most definitely wrong, and it was more than just nerves. My voice just wasn't working for some reason. All my usual vocal tricks made zero difference, and, well, the bottom line is, I did not make a good showing.

Mr. Gaither was very kind to me. He told me he appreciated me coming and that he would be in touch. He flew me home, and I didn't hear from him again until several years later when Avalon was asked to sing on one of their Gaither Homecoming videos. That whole experience was just another punch in the gut. Once again, it was like, *You suck, Jody. You're not good enough to do this.*

I decided to go to the vocal doctor because I could tell something wasn't right with my voice. I found out I had the beginning stages of a polyp on one vocal cord and the other cord looked strained. I was prescribed vocal rest and also encouraged to get vocal therapy. I didn't sing for several weeks.

I started wondering if perhaps I wasn't supposed to sing anymore. I figured I just needed to settle in California, find a job, and not expect to do anything professionally as a singer. After the Gaither tryout and then the vocal diagnosis, I had a bit of a mental breakdown. I went to a hotel, paid for a room for two nights, locked myself in, and just stared at the ocean and cried. I know, I know, it sounds so ridiculous, but I couldn't stop the emotions and the feeling of defeat. I was overwhelmed with the lack of direction.

So much of my identity was in singing. If I couldn't sing, who was I? I also couldn't control the emotions and how they were overwhelming me. I remember moments in that hotel when I thought, *Jody, you're being ridiculous. Grow up. Enough with the crying and whining.* But I couldn't shake it.

On top of everything, I was also a mess financially. I was running up credit card bills and spending money I didn't have, all while trying to cope with the feelings of emptiness inside of me.

I sat down with Gerald a few days later and told him everything I was thinking and feeling. Gerald wasn't an overly emotional kind of guy, and I can only imagine what a wreck I must have seemed like to him. However, he never made me feel that way. Finally, after we talked through everything that was going on, he recommended and even paid for me to see a counselor. He believed much more was going on than I understood or was willing to admit.

Time proved him more right than either of us realized.

EIGHT:
THE IMPETUS

My first counseling visit was like most counseling sessions—you talk, they listen. The hour is up, and on the next visit, you start unpacking things. Dr. Lynn, my counselor, was in her late 60s. From the moment I walked into her office, I felt like she had already read my mail. She was like a wise oracle, like Yoda, Dumbledore, or Laurence Fishburne from *The Matrix* (minus the red or blue pill). She was smart, quick-witted, and gentle. She asked all the right questions and dug deeply into places I had never spoken of—events I had swept under the rug of my soul and was afraid to ever bring out into the light—ever.

I explained to her how my emotions seemed to be out of control and how I understood that everyone has setbacks in life, but mine overwhelm me. I recognized my irrational behavior, but it was like a locomotive speeding down a steep hill, and I couldn't figure out how to stop it.

By the time our fourth session was over, through sobs and an ache I had never felt before, I admitted to her the darkest secret I'd ever kept—words that had never left my mouth. I had been sexually molested as a child.

I was paralyzed with fear about the entire ordeal. Even now as I type these words, I get chills. The struggle about whether or not to share this with the world was one I prayerfully considered for months. In fact, I placed this book on hold because I couldn't decide. Besides my wife, only two other people in the world knew about it. But I ultimately chose to include it because it's part of my story and it's something the enemy used to try to destroy me. I also chose to include it because childhood sexual abuse is something that is far more common than we care to think, and it is my deepest hope that my story will encourage someone with a similar secret to see that bringing these hurts out into the light is the first step in the healing process.

I was seven years old. *Seven!* I was taken advantage of by someone I trusted, an adult who was in a position of leadership over children—a Sunday school worker with a sterling reputation in the church, a close friend of my parents, and an upstanding member of the community.

It happened twice, once on the playground after Sunday evening service when I was led to believe we were going to swing on the swings. The second was in my own home while a church gathering was taking place in the next room. While I painfully remember enough to know it happened, a lot of the horrible details are a blur, something I have to believe was my seven-year-old brain's way of protecting me from what should never happen to anyone, let alone a child. Maybe the vagueness of my recollection is the Holy Spirit's way of protecting me.

Lynn listened, sitting next to me with kindness in her eyes, her arm around my shoulder and a box of tissues in her lap. I can't be certain, but I thought I even saw her eyes welling up with tears. I felt in that moment that I was going to physically fall apart and that my skin was the only thing holding me together.

After that session, I sat in my car in the parking lot and stared for a long time at the *H* on my steering wheel that stood for Honda. I didn't want to go back to my apartment. It was like I was seven years old again, and I didn't feel safe anywhere. I had blocked out all of it for so long, and now I was reliving it. I wasn't quite sure what to do or where to go, so instead of going back to my apartment, I drove straight to the Barneses' house. I needed to feel like I had a family. I needed to feel like I wasn't alone.

I don't recall anyone asking me why I randomly showed up. I just said, "Is it okay if I sleep here tonight?" Of course, as always, they gave me my old room.

I went back to see Lynn a few times over the next few weeks, and in her kindness, I was able to find some calm from the storm that had overwhelmed me.

It was nearly Christmas, and I planned on staying in California for the holidays. Dr. Lynn felt it might be best to have my parents come to a session with me so we could tell them together what had happened. I invited my parents to come to California just before Christmas.

I walked into that counseling room with both of my parents who were kind but timid like they were waiting for a bomb to go off and didn't know when it was going to explode or how big the explosion was going to be. Dr. Lynn sat next to me on the couch, and my parents sat in chairs across from us.

As I started to share with my parents why they were there and what had happened, my father became enraged, and tears filled his eyes. My mother was shocked and looked down in disbelief. Neither of them had any idea what had happened, and while they were both processing their feelings, they shared the overwhelming look of complete shock.

I know my parents well and love them enough to know that if they had known, they would have taken action immediately. Neither of them was aware that anything had ever happened. Why would they be? I was threatened by the perpetrator to never tell anyone or my father would lose his job and they would both be so disappointed with me that I would never be allowed to live with them again. So I was always terrified to tell them anything. I never said a word.

As I got older, I buried it deeply. Every time a thought tried to resurface, I started singing something or turned on music that distracted me. But when it first happened and for all the years after, I was humiliated and made to think it had all been my fault, that I had somehow done something to cause it. Lynn helped me put all the pieces together with my adult brain and see the entire, horrible ordeal for what it was. I was a victim, and it was a crime.

I know now that none of it was my fault. I was a child, for heaven's sake. I was prey. I was preyed upon by a sick, deranged individual. That was one of the things my father struggled with greatly. He took his responsibility as father and protector very seriously, and beyond his anger and desire for retaliation, there was a sense of great guilt because he didn't see the signs or wasn't able to protect me. I have never once felt that either of them needed to own any of the blame.

I've heard many people say, "How could God allow a child to be abused in such a way?" I have to admit, there have been times when I've wondered the same thing. Still, I think we have to remember that we live in a sinful world full of hurt, severely damaged people. I'm sure you've heard the old adage *Hurt people hurt people.* Most people who have been through trauma or abuse as children and have no proper guidance or any kind of positive reinforcement tend to lash out in horribly unhealthy ways as adults. It's not just unfortunate that it is so often children; it is abhorrent. But the older I get and as hard a pill as it is to swallow, I believe that nothing is wasted in the hands of Christ. I'm finally starting to see some glimmer of purpose in enduring that nightmare and somehow finding forgiveness for the one who caused it.

After we went through hours of exhausting and emotionally draining conversations with my counselor, my parents went back to the Barneses' house, where we spent the next few days together. We celebrated Christmas together as best we could. When it came time for my parents to leave, I was sad to see them go but also grateful that we'd had the opportunity to walk through it all together. They are and always have been a pillar of strength and support for me at some of the worst times in my life. But even though they always appeared to be strong and impervious, they are still human beings, and something like this had to affect them in a deep place. I know now as a parent that it would destroy a part of me to know my child had suffered helplessly at someone else's hand.

As the years passed, I watched the revelation of my abuse change my father, not in ways that anyone else could notice. He was always a gentle and kind man, but something in him grew sad toward me as though he felt pity or maybe guilt for something he hadn't done, regardless of how many times I assured him otherwise. I could always see it in his eyes, and I think the entire ordeal broke his heart far more than it broke mine.

* * *

The next few months of life chugged along as I worked retail and let my voice—and my heart—heal. And then one morning several months later, my phone rang. On the other end of the line was Roger Breland's brother, Billy. He was the bookkeeper and office manager for TRUTH and advisor and assistant to his brother. Half-awake, I grumbled hello into the receiver. "Jody? Bill Breland here. Did I wake you?"

"Well, yes, it's two hours earlier here."

Billy apologized. "Listen, I just wanted to let you know I'm ready for you to come back to TRUTH."

I chuckled a little at that sentence because although Billy was a big part of keeping TRUTH on the road, he had very little say regarding who came and went.

I told him I believed that chapter was closed for me.

"All I ask is that you think about it. TRUTH is going to be at Skyline Wesleyan in San Diego next week. You should drop in and see them. I'll talk to you soon." And then he hung up.

That weekend I drove down to San Diego. Two years had passed since I left like a ninja under cover of night. I honestly had no idea what to expect, but I knew, if nothing else, I would be able to apologize to JRB for leaving so abruptly.

I showed up a little before the concert started, and TRUTH was backstage praying before taking the stage. After the prayer, Roger looked up and saw me standing there. Without missing a beat, he said, "I thought you said you'd be right back." We both smiled, and immediately the situation was disarmed.

He was, as always, very kind to me. The group sounded amazing, and in my heart I missed being up there with them. I drove home that night with mixed emotions. I had a dream in my heart of being a professional singer. I wanted to tour and see the world. But I had come to grips with the fact that my season was probably over. I had so many scars—old ones and newly surfaced ones that had me feeling like I didn't have a place in the Christian music world. I knew how they liked their musicians, squeaky clean with sterling reputations. That was no longer me. And besides, I had started a whole new life in California, a life I was truly content with.

A month or so later on a Sunday afternoon, Roger called me. He told me that TRUTH was signing a record deal with Integrity Music and that he was putting together a new group. He wanted me to be part of that group. I was standing in front of what is now the chapel at Friends Church in Yorba Linda. The sun was shining, and the palm trees were gently swaying in the 72-degree breeze. My life in California was, for all intents and purposes, perfect. So my knee-jerk reaction was to say no. Besides, I worried about what it might be like to go back, what my parents would think, and what the Barneses would think.

Financially, I couldn't return for the meager wage that was standard for TRUTH members. Roger agreed to pay me more if I would agree to also be the road manager. I needed to think and pray about it, so I asked him for a little time.

I wrestled with what was the right thing to do. I loved my new life in California. I loved my friends and my new, extended family. But I also knew if I didn't get back on the road and start doing music again full-time I would never be able to fulfill my dream. TRUTH was my chance to move in that direction. I knew what I had to do.

A month or so later, I flew to Mobile, Alabama, to meet up with the TRUTH bus. That night, they were singing a concert at the University of Mobile. While I didn't sing with them until a few days later, Roger did call me onstage to sing my song "So Far, So Good." I met the new group that consisted of Jason Breland,

Natalie Grant, Michelle Pitzer (Swift), Janna Potter (Long), and Brad Parsley. These folks are all powerhouse vocalists, and as I listened to all of them sing that night, I knew this was going to be a TRUTH like no other.

As much as I'd like to say I was finally totally and completely focused on the Lord's calling for my life and what my true purpose was, that wouldn't be true. It was still about the dream of being a recording artist. It was about traveling the globe and performing for thousands of people. It was about hearing my songs on the radio and playing those dream venues. I was more focused on myself and less on God.

I carried with me a deep loathing for myself and for my past, both the situations that were my fault and those that were not. All of it made me feel like a scarred, imperfect mess. To compensate for how I felt about myself internally, I poured myself into music, into the performance. I worked so hard to appear as though I had it all together and didn't need anyone's help. But inside, I wasn't fixed. I hadn't healed.

I was back on the road singing again full-time just like I always wanted to. I was hopeful that maybe this time I would be able to pull this off without anyone knowing how broken I really was.

NINE:
THE ENCORE

I joined TRUTH a second time, and it was not the TRUTH it had been in the past. Because we were signed to a new recording label, there was a definitive push to have a more relevant and current sound. They chose a young rock producer named Paul Mills to helm the next project, and in the summer of 1995, the group went into the studio and began working on the record *One*.

The style and sound of *One* was very different from the previous TRUTH albums. It was shaping up to be a pop album in every sense of the word. The typical TRUTH sound of singing on the breath was replaced with a vastly more aggressive group vocal sound. It must have been a real stretch for Roger Breland when he heard some of the rough mixes. He never let on that it was, but I can imagine he felt like he might be risking the loss of decades of TRUTH fans with this new sound. To this day, I listen back to the *One* album and think, *Why are we screaming?*

When the album finally released in 1996, it was met with mixed reviews. Some loved the new sound and raved about how much they had wanted TRUTH to move in this direction. Others felt it was too much and not true to the signature sound the group was known for. With churches and worship leaders being the core audience for TRUTH, there was an obvious struggle booking the group, knowing it would be carrying this new sound and repertoire. All the singers, me included, really loved the record and were jazzed about doing something different. We looked forward to any chance we got to sing the songs live.

Unfortunately, the record was not as well received as both Integrity and JRB had hoped. We didn't end up using much material from that album in our live concerts and instead sang hits from previous years. One of the songs I sang was "The Mind of Christ." We ended up putting that song into the permanent concert rotation. It had incredibly beautiful lyrics, and I loved singing it every night.

One positive thing about recording a true pop record was that it gave me the chance to hone some of my pop vocal skills. When I was in Los Angeles, I started to experiment and work with different vocal styles and found that my voice naturally gravitated toward the pop sound, probably because I was influenced by what I was listening to—artists like Mariah Carey and Whitney Houston, both who seldom sang a straight line. It was a lot of what we call runs (or licks back in the day). I had started to train my voice to be able to do some of that. The *One* album gave us all the opportunity to work on some of those techniques.

That runny, licky, soulful pop sound was just where music was at the time and where my singing style gravitated. Most of the other TRUTH singers had the same soulful sound. Natalie Grant was one of those who had a strong, pop sound. She also had an amazing high-whistle tone going on, much like Mariah. Michelle also had a very unique and contemporary pop sound (brilliant singer, amazing tone). Then there was Janna Potter. For whatever reason, she made us all sound like second-rate musicians. She had soul that came from her bones (and still does). It was a polished, professional sound that usually didn't happen in someone so young and inexperienced. She wasn't a "runny" singer, not because she couldn't do it, but because she sounded more like the classic, soulful singers of days gone by such as Aretha Franklin, Gladys Knight, and Anita Baker Her voice was as smooth as silk.

At that point, the group was being pushed as a legitimate, signed artist. I don't ever want to delegitimize anyone's work, but there is a difference between an artist signed to a label, supported and solicited, and a touring music group with no label support behind them. For example, a radio station is not going to play a song from somebody who isn't signed. They've got to have the support of a record label. Having Integrity Music behind us opened several doors that TRUTH would not normally have been able to walk through.

Each year, the Gospel Music Association (GMA) hosted an event called Seminar in the Rockies in Estes Park, Colorado. Shortly after *One* was released, TRUTH was asked to be the house band for a showcase night at Estes Park. The primary purpose of the week-long event was to give new, up-and-coming singers and songwriters a place to learn how the music industry works, as well as a place for some of them to showcase their talents. Many well-known artists and songwriters were discovered at Seminar in the Rockies. Representatives from all the major Christian labels attended, seeking to sign the next big thing to a record deal or a songwriter to a publishing deal.

TRUTH arrived in Colorado and rehearsed our set with the band, and then the band rehearsed all the other music they would be playing for other artists. A couple singers and I had the responsibility of hosting the artist showcase that evening. Each of us was responsible for keeping the evening moving and introducing the artists before they performed.

When it came time for me to introduce an artist, I took to the stage and hyped up the crowd. The entire time I was thinking, *What was the name of the group I'm introducing?* As the group started to take the stage behind me, I had stalled for as long as I possibly could and *still* could not remember their name. Because it was starting to get awkward, I said, "This next group is taking the gospel music world by storm. Put your hands together, and make them welcome!" Then I ran off the stage, humiliated. When their first song was over, one of the singers stepped up and said, "My name is Ben Issacs, and we are the Issacs."

Backstage I was like "The Issacs! Shoot!"

Fast-forward to 2020. I was at a special CCM event and had the chance to talk to the Issacs personally. They didn't remember what happened, or at least they said they didn't. They were probably just being nice, but we had a good laugh, and I was able to apologize for not paying closer attention.

Sitting in the audience that night was a guy named Grant Cunningham. He was the head of A&R (Artist and Repertoire) for Sparrow Records—now Capitol Christian—that was EMI Christian Music Group back then. He had been looking for specific vocalists for a mixed pop quartet Sparrow wanted to put together. Apparently, he heard something he liked because he was hanging around after the evening was done to talk to Janna. I wish I could say that Grant came up to me as well, but he did not. He approached Janna and introduced himself. He'd seen something special in her, most likely the same thing all of us saw in her. He told her about how they were starting a new pop group and asked if she would be interested in being part of it.

The name of the group had already been chosen—Avalon. They had two guys who were already committed to the group, as well as a female singer. They just needed one more strong, female vocalist to round out the group, and Janna was destined to be just that.

Janna and I had become good friends while singing together in TRUTH. This TRUTH group was close-knit, but as I said before, there are always personality and relational issues, especially when you have six highly talented singers traveling together. Egos can get out of control, and at times jealousy can be a problem. Janna was always a very confidant person, not easily ruffled by what other people thought or said about her. But I knew she was struggling with some personality issues in the group and getting tired of the drama. Actually, many of us were starting to grow weary, and it was becoming more of a struggle for us to maintain the commitment we made to JRB and Integrity.

Janna talked to me about Sparrow's offer. She was obviously excited but didn't know what to do. My first reaction was not jealousy but more disappointment. We had both made this commitment to TRUTH and to the record company. It was hard for me to see her go, and at first I struggled with her decision. But it was an amazing opportunity for her, and I knew that.

She decided to accept the position with Avalon but was scared to tell JRB. She sneaked away to Nashville on her days off for meetings, and we would all cover for her. But the time was drawing nearer for her to have to be in Nashville full-time. She had to tell JRB what was going on, and he was not happy.

I always believed Janna was bigger than TRUTH. I thought the same about Natalie Grant and many of the others I shared the TRUTH stage with. That's not meant to be a slam on TRUTH in any way. TRUTH served an incredible purpose, which was to establish Christian artists and musicians by giving them a forum and a crash course in living on the road. It was truly like boot camp for artists and musicians.

That doesn't mean it was easy for B when someone left the group to pursue their Nashville dreams. And I'm sure it was even harder for him when they were wooed away by music industry bigwigs. I know he always wanted TRUTH to be more than it was. I think the older he got, the more he realized that his gift was being a cultivator and mentor.

He always had the uncanny ability to find incredibly talented people who hadn't been trained and teach them how to become a professional. The interesting thing is that he is still doing that to this day. He is cultivating young talent at the University of Mobile, shaping them into excellent performers with whole hearts for worship. There is no doubt in my mind that this was his calling from the beginning.

After Janna left the group, it hurt me more than I realized. As dramatic as it sounds, I felt like she had abandoned me. She was my duet partner, and we had a great time together on the road. But TRUTH continued without her, and I resigned myself to do so as well.

Janna had invited all of us to come and see them perform on a Christmas tour called the Farewell Young Messiah Tour. TRUTH happened to have the night off, so we rented a car and drove to St. Louis to see the show. I was truly happy for her and never prouder than when we got to see her perform for the first time with Avalon.

At that time, Avalon was made up of Rikk Kittleman, Michael Passons, Tabitha Fair, and Janna. The concert was a multi-artist event with CeCe Winans, Steven Curtis Chapman, Carman,

4Him, Point of Grace, Twila Paris, and several others. It was a huge platform for Avalon, and we were blown away by their performance.

As I watched Avalon perform that night, I thought, *Janna is living my dream. This is my dream!* I wondered if that was ever going to happen for me.

Avalon's sound was beyond current—it was fresh, modern, and unlike anything on CCM radio at that time. Even the way they were dressed was over-the-top. That night, it was obvious that this group was something special. I remember leaning over to someone while Avalon was singing and saying, "They're going to be huge." You could tell that this was the vibe in the massive crowd as well, and everyone else could feel it too.

We left that night thrilled for Janna and excited for what was ahead for her. We got back on the TRUTH bus the next day and started traveling again, but for days, the thought of Avalon and what I had seen stayed with me. As the days and weeks passed, I moved on and focused on my commitment to TRUTH.

TEN:
THE GOLDEN OPPORTUNITY

We finished our Christmas tour and took a short break
to be with our families. In the new year, we flew to
Mobile to rejoin the group. We immediately dove
back into concert dates, and thoughts of Avalon and Janna started
to fade as the schedule and life on the bus became more hectic.

The next few months were a struggle relationally. Everyone
worked hard to keep the group together and get along with one
another, but there was one member who consistently seemed to
cause drama and stir up conflict. Every member at one time or
another had a confrontation with this person, and it was taking
a toll on everyone. As I've stated before, you cannot live on a
bus with 15 people and not have confrontation, but this was
going above and beyond that. It was antagonistic and toxic, and
it always seemed to revolve around that one person. Most of the
people on the bus were beyond frustrated with it, and I was one
of them.

In late February 1996, Janna called me. She asked if I was still happy out on the road and if I would ever consider leaving. After we discussed much of the drama and obvious answers to those questions, I asked her to cut to the chase. She said, "One of the guys that was going to be in the group didn't work out. Would you want to come and audition for that position?"

My first response was, "No, I can't do that to JRB. I can't do that to the group." Her response was, "Okay, well, I'm just telling you, this is going to be a really big deal, and I want you to come and be part of it. If you change your mind, let me know because we're looking for a strong male singer, and we need someone sooner rather than later."

I was torn between my commitment to TRUTH and JRB and my desire to fulfill the next level of my dream. The abrupt way I'd left the group the first time weighed heavily on me as well. I presented the idea to my parents and the Barneses, and they both responded with "Jody, you have to do this! This is what you've always wanted to do. An opportunity like this may never come around again." Everyone was on the same page but me. I continued to struggle with the decision. I felt I had hurt JRB so much in the past, and I just couldn't bring myself to do that to him again.

With apprehension, I called Janna and told her I was willing to audition and see how I felt afterward. That meant I would have to sneak around like she had and keep it all a secret, which ratcheted up my anxiety. On my next available day off, I made some excuse about having to fly home, and Sparrow Records and Grant Cunningham flew me to Nashville to audition and meet with the other members of Avalon.

At that time, Sparrow—its parent company was EMI—was the most successful Christian label in the industry. As I pulled up to the building in Brentwood, Tennessee, my heart began to pound hard in my chest. *This isn't real. This isn't happening.* Someone escorted me to a waiting area in the lobby. As I waited, I looked around. On the walls surrounding me were large photographs of all the artists currently on the Sparrow-EMI roster. Artists like BeBe and CeCe Winans and Steven Curtis Chapman smiled back at me, and my hands started to sweat. *Maybe this is too much for me. Maybe I'm not good enough to be here.* Gulp.

So many of these artists I had looked up to my entire life were on that wall. My stomach sank, and I suddenly felt sick, but before I could run away, the tall, smiling, freckle-faced Grant Cunningham walked through the door and shook my hand. "Hello, Jody. We're so glad you're here. Welcome to Sparrow Records."

Grant and I talked for a long time. He played some songs for me that were chosen for Avalon's new record. We discussed the songs Janna had played for him of me singing (one of them was "The Mind of Christ"), and he was very complimentary. He told me he had been impressed with me that night in Estes Park, but at the time, he wasn't in need of a male vocalist. He asked me a thousand questions, and I'm sure my answers were fumbled and less than adequate, but Grant always had a way of putting a person at ease. He was always kind. He had a larger-than-life personality and looked like a six-foot, body-building Opie from *The Andy Griffith Show*. I speak about Grant in the past tense because he passed away unexpectedly in 2002 while playing in an over-30 soccer league. He was a brilliant husband, father, songwriter, and friend, and his death was a blow to all of us.

After we spent a few hours talking, listening to music, and singing a bit, Grant asked me if I would be interested in being part of something like Avalon, and I told him I thought I might. I was honest about how difficult it would be to break my commitment to TRUTH, but I understood the opportunity, and if it were presented, I didn't want to let it pass me by.

We left Sparrow and drove to lunch to meet up with the three current members of the group—Michael, Tabitha, and Janna. We all got along well that day, and I was impressed by how established and grounded all of them seemed. After lunch, someone drove me back to the airport, and I flew back to meet TRUTH in Illinois.

About a week later, TRUTH had a day off in Kansas City, and I was in a hotel room with Brad Parsley. We seldom got to sleep in and rarely in a bed that wasn't moving down the freeway. Brad and I had decided to take full advantage of the day off to sleep in and rest. Around 9:00 a.m., our room's phone rang. I answered on the third ring, still half-asleep, and said, "Yeah?"

It was Grant Cunningham on the other end. "Hi, Jody, it's Grant. Did I wake you?" I told him he had but it was only because we had a day off and never get to sleep in. He laughed and said, "Well, I'll let you enjoy your rest and your day off, but I wanted to call and extend an invitation for you to join Avalon and become a Sparrow Records recording artist. Is that something you would be interested in?"

I can't remember exactly what my response was, but it was something like, "Does the Pope wear a funny hat? Yes! Yes! Yes! Thank you so much."

"Jody, we are so excited to have you," he said. "Welcome aboard. I'll be in touch soon."

Brad was in the other bed staring at me. He was in the know about everything and was as excited about the phone call as I was. When I hung up, Brad asked, "What did he say? What did he say?" I stood up on my bed and shouted, "I'm the newest member of Avalon," and started jumping up and down. We celebrated most of the day, and I'm pretty sure I didn't stop smiling. I remember calling my parents and telling them about it, and they were both very proud. I'm pretty sure my dad cried. It wasn't until later in the day that I felt the weight of the difficult conversation I needed to have with Roger Breland.

Roger didn't always travel with us on the road, but he did happen to be with us that weekend. By this point, he was aware that something was brewing with me, Nashville, and Avalon. However, he also thought that things were still up in the air and nothing had been confirmed. The next morning, we checked out of the hotel, and it happened to be my turn to drive the bus. I pulled it up to the front of the hotel, and TRUTH members began coming aboard.

I had seen JRB in the lobby the day before and told him we needed to talk at some point. I think he knew what was coming. He was the last one to board the bus and sat on the jump seat next to the driver in the front. He pulled the curtain closed between the driver and the rest of the bus and then turned to me and said, "Okay, what's going on?"

I told him about the early-morning phone call the day before and the invitation to join Avalon. Then I told him I had accepted. He simply said, "Okay." He hopped up, opened the curtain, walked to his back office, kicked everybody out, shut the door, and did not come out until we arrived at our destination.

It was almost two months later when I left TRUTH to move to Nashville. JRB and I didn't talk about it until the week before I left. He was quiet, and there was definitely a chill between us, but he was never unkind. I imagine he was hurt because his group was falling apart, and he couldn't do anything about it. How was he going to explain to Integrity Music that he was losing another one of his singers? In hindsight, I can see that it must have put him in a very difficult position.

Right before I left the group, I flew to Nashville to be part of a New Artist Showcase during Gospel Music Association week. GMA week was a huge deal back in the '90s. Record companies hosted artists, radio stations, publishers, and anyone who was in any way involved in Christian music. That year happened to be the 20th anniversary of Sparrow Records, and Avalon was a featured artist in the New Artist Showcase.

The timing was interesting because TRUTH drove to Memphis from Little Rock that morning. They had a day off and were going to perform at Bellevue Baptist Church the next day, so it worked out geographically. Sparrow flew me in from Arkansas, I sang on the GMA New Artist Showcase that day, and then drove to Memphis to be with TRUTH that night. It also happened that we were close enough to Nashville that JRB could audition new singers for my soon-to-be-vacant position.

When I arrived at the church in Memphis, singers were going on and off the stage auditioning for my part. I sat in the back of this massive church and listened to them sing. They were all really great singers, and any of them could have done well in my position. I caught JRB's eye, and he just looked annoyed. I'm fairly certain it was because he didn't want to be in this position to begin with.

B had a love-hate relationship with the Nashville recording industry. Over the years, he had watched them take many of his singers away. He warned us to be careful because of how viscous the record industry could be. Nevertheless, so many of his singers had left for Nashville with the hopes of getting a record deal. It was the dream of just about everyone who rode that bus, and many of them succeeded.

Regardless of how frustrated he felt that he had to replace me, I want to reiterate that he was never unkind to me. I would like to think that maybe deep down he was proud of me. Up to that point, he had been such an important part of my story and had walked with me through so much. I saw Christ in him in many ways. No matter how many times I did something to disappoint him, he always forgave me and gave me another chance. I have always appreciated that. I probably wouldn't be where I am if not for the grace Roger Breland showed me.

As my last day with the group approached, JRB and his son Jason took me to dinner to say farewell. They gave me a Rolex watch with the dates of my time in the group engraved on the back. It was like he was giving me his blessing to move on, and that watch has always meant the world to me.

The move to Nashville was overwhelming. I was so excited to start this new chapter in my life, and I had an optimistic view of what life as a professional recording artist would be like. Although I had not technically signed a contract yet with Avalon and Sparrow Records, I had a verbal commitment that it was happening, and that was enough for me. Though the management and representation at the record label was amazing, no one took the time to tell me what to expect when I moved to Tennessee. I guess they just thought I was an adult and should know. Yeah, right.

At the time, I didn't have a car. Since I was a recording artist now and no doubt would be rolling in it soon, I decided to lease a new car and pay for it with all the money I was about to make. I went to the Volkswagen dealership and leased a brand-new VW Jetta, all on my own.

What I didn't realize until I had been in Nashville for a couple of weeks and after several meetings with the record company was that we didn't have a source of income until we started touring. Once we finally signed our contracts, there was a small advance we had to split four ways. After taxes, that was a little more than $1,200 for each of us. My car payment alone each month was $400, so it didn't take long to blow through that money and realize, *Wow! I need to get a job.*

I ended up working at a Kroger grocery store stocking shelves after hours and working in the children's section of a department store in the evenings. During the daytime hours, Avalon was in the studio working on their debut release. When we weren't in the studio during the day, I also worked as the host for a popular restaurant in downtown Nashville.

For our debut release, Sparrow, Grant, and our manager, Norman Miller, wanted someone who had an eclectic and artsy perspective to produce it. For that task, they called on the talents of singer, songwriter, and producer Charlie Peacock. He had already built an amazing career as a recording artist and had a creative gift that was vastly different from the standard CCM projects being released at that time.

We recorded all the vocals at Charlie's home studio in Bellevue, Tennessee, just outside Nashville. He had purchased and converted an old church into a home and built a studio next to it. We had to walk through what seemed like a wild English garden in order to get to the studio. It was a very inspiring and almost magical place to make a record, like we were recording in the English countryside.

Charlie's process was, well, slow. He created as we went along. We all jumped in and out of the vocal booth trying different sounds until he found the right one for each song. After the first week, Janna, Tabitha, Michael, and I were getting along well and starting to craft a cohesive sound. Tabitha was already a well-established studio and session singer in Nashville and made a substantial living doing backup vocals and studio sessions for various country and Christian artists. It seemed like we often had to schedule Avalon's vocal sessions and recording times around her sessions. I don't remember anyone having an issue with that because we all knew it was how she made her living.

About three weeks into the recording process, we were all in the studio working. It was Michael's turn in "the box" to record a lead vocal. Janna was sitting on a large, black leather sofa in the back of the studio filing her nails, and I was sitting at the computer playing Tetris to pass the time. Tabitha was at the opposite end of the couch when her cell phone rang.

While I continued to stare at the Tetris game, I listened to Tabitha's phone conversation. She sounded excited and panicked. She kept saying, "Okay! Yes! Yes! I totally understand that! I will come right now. Of course. No problem. See you soon!" After she hung up the phone, she jumped up and announced to the room that she had to run out for a bit for a quick meeting on Music Row but that she would be back. Charlie understood, and Tabitha grabbed her bags and hurried out the door, saying, "See y'all later!"

I said bye as she walked out the door and then turned back to my game of Tetris. As I stared at the screen, I said to the silent studio, "Y'all, she ain't comin' back." That surprised the others, and they all just chuckled. We didn't see Tabitha again for nearly two years.

Tabitha was being courted by other record companies to do a solo pop record, something that was probably a personal dream of hers. She was most likely told that day that if she signed and went through with recording the Avalon record, she wouldn't be able to have a solo deal. She is such a gifted musician and a wonderful person that I don't think being part of Avalon was what she expected. When faced with the decision, she chose to leave. We all understood, and no one begrudged her for doing so, but it left us without a soprano singer, and the recording process was suddenly put on hold.

The night after Tabitha left, our manager, Norman Miller, took us to dinner to give us a bit of a pep talk. He had a thick Scottish accent and an unshakable positivity. He encouraged us, saying we would find another singer and the record would move forward as planned.

In the meantime, Michael, Janna, and I had very little money and now more time on our hands. Michael was still traveling occasionally and leading worship at church youth camps. Financially, he was a little bit better off than Janna and me. I actually lived with Michael and slept on his couch for the first three months I was in Nashville. Janna would come over, and we would combine groceries and cook what we had. There was a lot of red beans and rice and not much else.

Michael's place was a small, one-bathroom flat that really wasn't meant for two bachelors. I needed to find my own place to live, something I could afford on my own with the little money I was making. Through word of mouth, I found an apartment not far from where Michael and Janna lived that was only $500 a month. It was tiny, it was old, but it was perfect for just me and even came with a washer and dryer. It was in a house that had been divided into five apartments. It had a tiny kitchen, a living area, a small bedroom, and an even smaller bathroom.

There was a door-shaped hole in the middle of the living area that led to a miniature basement and laundry room. If you ran into the house too quickly, you risked tumbling straight down those steps and breaking your neck. It was a strange setup for sure, but it was cheap, and I made it as comfortable as possible.

Eventually, I found someone who rented that basement bedroom—we called it "the cave"—as a place to crash. He worked as a crew guy on various music tours and was seldom home. We split the rent. He paid $200, and I paid $300. I paid more since

I had the "real" bedroom with the bathroom. I was fine having a roommate because I needed every penny to survive, and splitting the rent helped—not to mention we had a great time and a lot of laughs.

Because the recording process was delayed and taking much longer than expected, I was working 300 jobs and still couldn't make enough money to cover all my expenses. I couldn't afford to pay for my car anymore, but I had signed a lease. My only hope was to find someone honest who would sublease the car and take over the payments. I have no idea how I found someone, but I did, and they took over my payments. However, that left me without a car, and I still needed transportation to get to all my jobs. My parents came to my rescue and gave me their old car—a 1995 Plymouth Acclaim. It was white with red velour interior, so I affectionately named it Red Velvet. It only had an AM/FM radio, so I improvised by strapping a boombox to the front dashboard.

If I took a sharp, left-hand turn too quickly, water poured from behind the dash onto the feet of whoever was sitting in the passenger seat. I used to love it when Janna rode with me. She always complained about not having a CD player, so I would just make a sharp left and shut her up. Stephanie and I were dating at that time, and her dad wouldn't let me park the car in front of their house because it leaked oil so badly and would ruin their driveway. It wasn't the most luxurious car, but it was free and dependable, minus the flood and oil spotting, so I was grateful for it.

With all these pieces falling into place, I finally began to settle into my new life as a Nashvillian. Avalon still didn't have a female singer to take Tabitha's place, and I was barely making enough money to eat, but I knew it was where I needed to be, and for the first time in a very long time, I was happy.

ELEVEN:
THE DREAM

Nikki Hassman became the newest member of Avalon. She was a young, spunky, talented singer with killer vocal chops, and she was a great songwriter to boot. Nikki had recently graduated from Belmont University in Nashville. Grant Cunningham approached her to see if she had any interest in being our newest member.

In hindsight, I'm fairly certain that Nikki only saw Avalon as a stepping-stone to bigger opportunities. But she agreed to join the group and brought with her a youthful spark and pop sound that rounded out the group blend perfectly. With Nikki on board, we were able to finish the first record quickly, and everyone, including the label, was very pleased with the result.

Norman Miller was scouting out a place to plug Avalon in as an opening act. His management company, Proper Management, looked over a huge roster of CCM artists, and one of them was Twila Paris. Also a Sparrow recording artist, Twila had just finished a new record and was about to begin touring. The only problem was that the tour was leaving in the fall, and our record wasn't slated to release until later that winter.

Usually when an opening act, or support act, as they're called, is put on a tour, it's because the act has newly launched their career and can bring some extra ticket sales. The record label would kick in some tour support dollars to help promote their new artist. Since Avalon wasn't established yet, we didn't have a whole lot but our voices to offer and a little tour support money from Sparrow.

Twila finally agreed to let us tag along on the tour if we agreed to sing backup for her. Norman thought it was a good idea because it would help create a buzz for the upcoming release, so we went along with it. Essentially, we were the opener for the opener. The father-son band Aaron Jeoffrey was the official opening act before Twila took the stage, and we went on before them and sang a couple songs from our new project.

We were all grateful to Twila for allowing us to join the tour, but we learned very quickly that there was more to singing backup than we all thought. During rehearsals for Twila's portion of the program, we were told there would be a musical interlude that was supposed to take you through every changing season. Whoever was responsible for her staging and choreography thought it would be a great idea for us to dance through the aisles during the musical moment that represented autumn and throw fake leaves on the audience on our way to the stage.

I still have a vivid memory of the tour meeting when this was described to us. I'm fairly certain our blank expressions spoke volumes to them as they were telling us what they wanted us to do. As we walked backstage, Michael said in his Mississippi twang, "I'll sing, and I'll even dance a little, but I ain't throwin' no leaves." We laughed at him and how he said it, but we all felt the same way.

In the end, we did it once or twice with Twila's sisters who were on tour with us, but it didn't go over quite like the organizers had hoped, so they nixed the idea. I'm assuming it was because people didn't like being pelted with leaves. I'm fairly certain that the ladies were scattering the leaves in the air delicately while Michael and I were throwing big handfuls at people. It wasn't as magical as they had hoped, and we were relieved that the idea died.

This was our first real tour experience, and we were actually getting paid to be out there, which was nice. It wasn't much, but we were grateful, and Twila really didn't have to do it. Her tour was on a tight budget and didn't have a lot of money to spare, but she was sweet and did it anyway. Again, we were all very grateful to her.

In the middle of that tour, our first single, "Give It Up," was released to the radio. Within a week, it went to number one, and the buzz for Avalon started growing very quickly.

Norman was well-known for putting huge, multi-artist Christmas tours together. He was responsible for the Young Messiah Tour where Avalon made their debut and where I had gone with TRUTH to hear them the year before. However, that tour was branded the farewell tour for Young Messiah, and Norman had to come up with something new. With the help of Sparrow Records, he created a new, multi-artist recording project and a tour called Emmanuel.

The tour featured artists Michael W. Smith, Twila Paris, 4Him, Point of Grace, Larnelle Harris, CeCe Winans, Anointed, Susan Ashton, and several others. Norman also invited Avalon to be part of Emmanuel because of the obvious promotional benefit. By the time the Emmanuel tour launched the day after Thanksgiving, and thanks to the strong success of the first single, people were starting to become familiar with Avalon.

Music on the radio at the time had a heavy rock influence. Everything was guitar-driven, and we were just starting to phase out of the grunge era. All of a sudden, there was this Avalon song with a euro-pop, dance groove. One of the songs actually had sirens in it. It was strange hearing it on the radio in the middle of everything else that was being played, but I also think that's why it was so successful. It was that fresh, new sound that Christian radio needed.

I will never forget it. My (now) wife and I were driving in downtown Nashville enjoying a date night. I had heard that our new single was on the local radio station, but I hadn't heard it yet. We had gotten back in the car after dinner and were heading down the road when Stephanie turned on the Christian radio station. The moment she did, we heard the DJ say, "Coming up next, the new single from the group Avalon." It was about to be the first time I had ever heard my voice on the radio.

I don't recall if she was driving or if someone else was, but I do remember sticking my head out the sunroof when the song was playing and yelling at the top of my lungs to people we were passing on the street, "Hey, I'm on the radio! My song is being played on the radio!" People were whooping and clapping for me. It was an amazing moment, one I had been waiting for my entire life.

A couple of months after that, we were being introduced on the Emmanuel tour. We were the last artist in the lineup of very successful artists. Twila and Steven Curtis Chapman introduced the artists every night. Twila asked if she could be the one to introduce us since we had been on tour with her.

She said, "Ladies and gentlemen, it's my honor to introduce a new group to you that I've been on tour with this past fall. Their first single went straight to number one, and their album is at the top of the charts right now." Before she could finish the introduction, people were going crazy. "Would you please make welcome—Avalon!" As I stood on that stage each night listening to the crowd's reaction, I thought, *Wow! This is really happening.*

When I look back on it, I often think about how much my perspective has changed and how I wish I could go back and tell that kid—me—some things. I wish I knew then what I know now about how necessary accountability is, how I needed to understand what kind of toll this level of exposure and chaotic schedule was about to take on my life and my body. In the moment, you don't think about those things. As a 26-year-old, all I was thinking was, *I've made it. I'm living out my dream.*

We finished the second leg of Twila's tour in the spring of 1997 and began doing promo and press tours to promote our first release. We ended up with four number-one songs from our first, self-titled record. That was more than anyone expected, and our record company was thrilled at the response from radio and retail.

Avalon became a common name on Christian radio and, with the success of the first album, solidified a place in the CCM industry. Booking requests for Avalon began to flow in, and concert crowds were increasing. We spent the better part of spring and summer doing one-off dates and promotional appearances.

Most of it was a blur of hotels and early-morning flights sprinkled with label meetings anytime we returned to Nashville. At one of these meetings in early summer, Sparrow and Norman dropped the idea that we would go into the studio late summer to record our sophomore release. They wanted to release something quickly to take full advantage of the wave we had been riding.

In that meeting, we were warned ahead of time about something called the sophomore slump. I had never heard this phrase before, but Norman explained how many artists who experience huge success with their debut release have nowhere near the same success with the second album. The sophomore record is a make-it-or-break-it determiner, and while Sparrow was very pleased with the performance of our first release, the true test would be how well the second one was received.

I left that meeting feeling that familiar pit growing in my stomach. I had become a master at ignoring it for the sake of appearances, but it was always there. It gnawed at me in times like this. It was a feeling of inadequacy. If we didn't deliver what was expected of us, I knew it was somehow going to be my fault. I was the weak link, and that would soon be obvious to everyone.

Sparrow tapped Charlie Peacock again to head up the record, but he would not be the day-to-day producer again. Charlie was in the beginning stages of starting his own imprint label and would only produce in an administrative capacity. He would oversee and make sure we were staying true to the Avalon sound, but for the actual vocal production and arranging, the reins were handed to Chris Harris.

I was already a big fan of Chris's work with artists like DC Talk, Amy Grant, and Anointed, so I knew we were in good hands. I loved Chris's production style and personality. He was witty and encouraging. I believe he was the person responsible for the initial Avalon sound, layering several vocal passes of various, alternate melodies. It could be extremely tedious at times, and there was a lot of jumping in and out of the box to see which voice was best suited for a specific part or lead vocal.

Most of the leads on each song were passed off to the four of us with each of us taking a verse or half of a verse. Michael and Janna would start a song, and maybe Nikki and I would sing the second verse, or maybe Janna would sing the lead on the chorus while Michael or I sang an alternate lead melody on top of her vocal. It was like a puzzle that took hours and hours to put together, but it became the signature sound for the group and what we affectionately started calling ear candy.

As we neared the wrap-up of the record, I'm not sure any of us knew what to think of what we had done, mainly because we had all sung so much and so many different tracks that we didn't understand how it was all going to come together or make any sense until it was all edited and comped.

While I loved most of the songs on the record, there was one song in particular that everyone thought was fantastic—everyone, that is, but me. I just wasn't feeling it. I didn't love the demo when we first heard it in the initial song meeting for the record. Everyone went crazy when we heard the demo at a label meeting. They all went on and on about how amazing it was, and Grant, the one overseeing the song list, obviously heard something in it that I certainly did not. So the song stayed on the list. Even when we were working on that song in the studio, it felt like a mess to me—so many parts going in so many different directions that I just couldn't hear what everyone else was hearing.

The recording portion was finished, and we sent the songs to be mixed. Avalon was performing at a festival in Pennsylvania when Grant called us and let us know he was going to send several of the final mixes to us for our approval. After our sound check, we sat in the back of the bus together and listened to the mixes of half the record. We were blown away at how that studio craziness and ear candy had been transformed.

Grant had written a couple of songs on the record, and one of those ended up being the title cut, "A Maze of Grace." As we walked off the bus, we were all excited about what we had heard. I said to Janna, "I love every song except 'Testify to Love.' It's probably my least favorite song on the record." I think she was surprised by that, but we never brought it up again.

Well, to say I was wrong would be an understatement. "Testify to Love" was the first single from *A Maze of Grace*, and it went on to break the record for the most consecutive weeks at number one. It connected with people in a way I've never seen a song do. To this day, when that song begins, people jump to their feet and sing every word at the top of their lungs. It became an anthem, a song of hope and inspiration for people. Youth choirs around the country and throughout the world were learning "Testify to Love" and doing choreography to it. It became the most performed song at music competitions and the most requested song on Christian radio.

One day, I was in our manager's office signing pictures and catching up on some business tasks. I was sitting near Glenda McNally, the person responsible for our day-to-day itinerary. She was a fantastic woman with a feisty demeanor and a solid reputation for not taking crap from anyone. She was on the phone pushing for Avalon to have better billing at Celebrate Freedom, a huge Fourth of July event put on by a Christian music radio station in Dallas, Texas. The person she was negotiating with on speaker phone wasn't budging.

After going back and forth for several minutes, that person said to Glenda, "Why should Avalon get that kind of billing?" Glenda said in her own dry, forceful way, "Okay, you want to know why Avalon deserves that billing? I'll tell you why. 'Testify to Love,' that's why." The man simply said, "Well, I see your point, Glenda," and that was it.

That song opened so many doors and allowed us opportunities we hadn't had before—chances to perform onstage with A-list artists in A-list venues. I admit that I still don't completely understand why. It isn't even close to being my favorite Avalon song. Don't get me wrong, I'm extremely grateful that it had the success and connection it did. I'm also always encouraged when

I hear thousands of people sing along to every word of it. It has taught me that it isn't so much how *I* feel about the songs I sing as much as it is about the people I sing them for. If it moves people, brings them closer to God, and gives them joy or healing, then that's fine with me.

At the GMA Dove Awards that year, we were nominated for Group of the Year, Artist of the Year, Inspirational Song of the Year for "Adonai," and Pop Song of the Year for "Testify to Love." We were blown away by all the recognition. In 1998, Avalon was awarded "New Artist of the Year" from the GMA, so the expectation was high in 1999 given the number of nominations and success of *A Maze of Grace*.

The night of the Dove Awards, two of our nominations were awarded in the pre-show. Both Inspirational and Pop Song of the Year awards were presented to us during that time, and we took home trophies in both categories. We were elated and overwhelmed.

That year, we were also invited to open the 30th Annual Dove Awards main telecast singing "Testify to Love." After the pre-telecast awards, Avalon and everyone around us were buzzing with excitement. We went to our dressing rooms and changed into our outfits for the main telecast. Glenda, Norman, and our publicist from Sparrow were so excited and proud that we had swept both categories in the pre-show. Glenda walked into the green room after we swept the pre-show and said, "Yes! We did it!" Avalon was definitely a team effort, and Glenda had worked so hard to get us where we were.

Once we were dressed, our publicist and the stage manager escorted us to the stage to take our places for the opening of the telecast. They placed us on a raised platform behind a backdrop that would lift into the air at the beginning of the show. A large, round screen with an image of a rotating earth was lowered behind us. Dancers with large pieces of fabric mimicked the ocean and lined up in front of our platform. Confetti canons were loaded, and we were warned that they would be fired off at the final note of the song.

We were behind a giant partition that separated us from the live audience that filled what was then the Gaylord Event Center, now the Bridgestone Arena in Nashville. As we sat and waited for the live telecast to start, we were all riding the high of what had happened so far, and the nervous excitement was almost electric. I turned to the group and said, "You guys, think about it. We won Song of the Year for *both* the pop and inspirational formats in the pre-show. How could we not win Group of the Year?" They all agreed, and we became giddy with excitement about what might possibly be ahead.

Our publicist was within earshot and came over before we started and said, "Break a leg." She apparently had overheard what I said about our chances of winning Group of the Year, and right as the stage manager yelled, "30 seconds!" our publicist turned to us and said, "I'm so sorry, you guys, but you didn't win Group of the Year—Point of Grace did."

We all looked at each other, and I'm certain the blood rushed out of my face. Just as she walked off the stage, we heard, "10 seconds!" The divider rose into the air, and 17,000 people were staring at us, waiting for the telecast to begin. We didn't even have time to collect our disappointment. We sang the opening number, smiles on our faces, knowing that we had lost the award that we were so sure we had won.

It's interesting to me that our publicist knew who the winners of the awards were before they were even announced. I always thought that information was kept top secret and sealed until it was announced. Apparently, that wasn't the case. That night, Point of Grace did, in fact, win Group of the Year, and they had not even released a record during that nomination period. Everyone was stunned, but what it came down to, and what it always comes down to, is voting blocks. The decks are stacked based on the number of votes a record company submits. I'm sure Avalon has also won a time or two because of that. It's not fair, and it's not a true representation of who deserves the award, but there you go.

I want to be clear. I love the women from Point of Grace. I always have. In fact, if we had to lose to someone, I'm glad it was them. Today, they are dear friends, and we have since toured with them. When we talk about that year at the Doves and laugh about it now, they agree with us that it seemed unfair. It's amazing how time changes your perspective, and what mattered so much at the time doesn't matter as much in the grand scheme of things.

By the time we performed on the Doves, Nikki Hassman had left the group, and Cherie Paliotta had joined us. Nikki was being courted by Tommy Motolla and Sony music to do a solo record. She really was a great singer and songwriter, and I think she had higher aspirations than doing just Christian music. Nikki and I always got along well and still stay in touch often to this day. She married Adam Anders and now lives with her beautiful family in California, where she has seen great success writing and producing music for film and television.

I don't begrudge Nikki for having higher aspirations. I've always had them too. I understood what it was like to be in TRUTH and want more and what it was like to be in California and want more. Nikki had a dream and a goal, and she felt she needed to pursue that. If I'm being forthright, it felt like she had one foot in and one foot out of Avalon, like she knew something better might happen. In Avalon, things weren't always smooth sailing for her relationally. She struggled to get along with both Janna and Michael at times and never seemed to be overly excited about being part of the group because of those challenges.

During the early stages of Avalon when I wasn't touring or recording with the group, I had very little social interaction and didn't know a lot of people in Nashville to hang out with. A friend of mine from college knew that and invited me to join her and her husband at church one Sunday. I didn't have many Sundays off at that point, but when I did, I figured I had better find a place to worship. She invited me to a church called New Song Christian Fellowship in Franklin, Tennessee. That Sunday, I stood with everyone else and listened to some of the most amazing worship I had ever heard in a church service. I will never forget how amazing the choir, worship team, and musicians were. I thought, *Is this how every church in Nashville is? All these killer musicians onstage together?*

At New Song, the worship pastor was Dave Williamson, who had been a composer and songwriter-musician in the Christian music industry for years. It is well-known that talent begets talent, so these amazing singers, session singers, and musicians all gravitated to this church. My friend, who is also a musician, sat with me in the second to the last row. There came a moment when the pastor asked us to turn around and shake hands with the people around us, and that's when I saw her. She had the most unbelievable blue-gray eyes I had ever seen. My friend knew her and introduced us. "Jody, this is my friend Stephanie Harrison. Stephanie, this is Jody McBrayer." I'm pretty sure I just shook her hand and smiled.

She was exotic-looking. I had always liked brunettes, and this girl whose hand I shook was a drop-dead gorgeous brunette. As I turned back around, I hoped that wouldn't be the last time I ran into Stephanie Harrison.

A few weeks later, I had another Sunday off, and I saw Stephanie again at church. This time, I asked her if she wanted to go to lunch. She actually said yes, so I took her to O'Charley's. (Hey, I was a struggling artist and didn't have a lot of money.) It also happened to be her birthday, so I'm almost certain I let her get dessert too. She was easy to talk to and had a fantastic sense of humor. Most of all, she didn't know anything about music or who I was. That was the beginning of our courtship.

Stephanie and I dated on and off for the next three years. We'd get together, break up, get together, break up. She had a difficult time adjusting to being in a relationship with someone who was on the road, and I was struggling trying to manage a relationship and a new, quickly growing career. To be quite honest, I was so focused on my career and what was next for Avalon that I didn't know how to think about anyone or anything else.

The year Avalon was nominated for a Dove Award as New Artist of the Year, I asked Stephanie to be my date at the awards show. We were in an awkward stage of breaking up and then trying to figure out whether or not we wanted to get back together. I cared for her very much but just hadn't been very good at showing it or balancing relationship with career. Somewhat reluctantly, she agreed to join me. I found out much later that she actually had plans to break up with me permanently after the evening ended. She had also taken a small, glass dove from her grandmother's house and was going to present it to me if we didn't win the award.

That night, Avalon won, much to our surprise. When I got up to walk to the stage and accept the award, I hugged Stephanie and then followed Janna and Michael. I was thinking more about Stephanie than the award we had just won. As we took to the microphone, each of us thanked people who had helped us get there.

While I shared, I looked down at Stephanie, and she was smiling back at me. I saw those beautiful blue eyes and knew in my heart I had fallen in love and that she was going to be my wife. Everyone else was enamored by the win, but I was overwhelmed by the realization that in the audience was the girl I would spend the rest of my life with. I couldn't think about anything else.

As we went backstage and got on a golf cart to go to the press room, everyone was screaming, whooping, and hollering about winning, and I was thinking, "I'm going to marry that girl."

She told me later that since Avalon won, she didn't want to be a downer and end our relationship that night. I didn't ask her right away to marry me, and I did have to do a little damage control with her family in order to start dating her seriously again. We'd broken up so many times that her parents, rightfully so, were hesitant about our getting back together, let alone making a permanent commitment.

I decided to write them a letter and try to explain where my heart was and how serious I was about their daughter. I wrote, "I love your daughter. If you'll give me a chance, I'll show you just how much."

We got engaged several months later. We were engaged nine months and then got married on March 27, 1999. I was 29 years old; she was 24. We were young, and just like the cliché says, we didn't really know anything about life. But I knew I loved her. About that there was never any question. She was my match in every way and still is all these years later.

The memory of our wedding is like looking through a blurry, fairy-tale-type filter. We had an evening wedding, and the church was packed with family, close friends, and even some people who thought it would be fun to crash the wedding of one of the guys from Avalon. Obviously, we had great musicians and singers.

The members of Avalon sang along with our close friend Crystal Lewis who we had been on tour with at the time. Another friend, Marcia Ware Wilder, agreed to sing the Twila Paris song "How Beautiful." We asked Twila to sing it, but she graciously declined and said she only sings for family weddings now because so many people have asked. She was there, though, and told us later that when the song began, she slowly slid behind a column because she was so embarrassed she wasn't singing it. Marcia tore the song up, and I'm sure that didn't help Twila's embarrassment.

After the service, the reception was chaos. We held it at a popular hotel in downtown Nashville, and as coincidence would have it, a large, Christian college was also holding an event there. They were more interested in all the CCM artists in the hotel than they were their own event. Most of them crashed our reception, ate our food, and partied with our people. They ate all the groom's cake before I got a slice. Vultures! Anyway, Stephanie and I left 24 hours later for our honeymoon in Hawaii. We were excited about starting our life together.

TWELVE:
THE BREAKING

For most newlyweds, the first year is tough. When you're a traveling musician, well, let's just say it was a lot harder than either of us expected. But it was especially difficult for Stephanie. For obvious reasons, she hated being home alone while I was on the road. She was newly married and wanted to live out her life daily with her new husband, one that sadly was seldom home. Back then, I didn't have a choice. Being on the road was my job, and I was still extremely focused on my career.

We had several arguments about our life and whether or not she had made the right decision marrying someone like me. Even her mother and grandmother told her, "You knew what you were getting into before you married him. You knew he was a musician." But when you're in love, you make decisions based on your feelings; you don't necessarily think through what life is going to be like in a practical sense. No one wants to hear someone speak rationale when talking about affairs of the heart.

I don't blame Stephanie for being disappointed by how things were that first year. I don't think either one of us thought we'd made a mistake. But maybe she did think, *This is not what I thought marriage was going to be like.* We worked through it, but not because I was extremely flexible. We worked through it because Stephanie was strong and fought through her emotions to a place of understanding and acceptance. She has always been strong that way.

We got a puppy (Ella) to keep her company, and because she didn't like being alone in the house while I was gone, she and Ella stayed with her parents when I wasn't in town. We did the best we could to get through the first year, and overall we were very happy. I was thankful that God had allowed me to marry someone so patient. She was and always will be my best friend.

That first Christmas as newlyweds, we drove down to Florida to spend time with my mom, dad, and brothers. The brothers' gift to our mom and dad was a trip to Europe the following February, and they were excited. When my father was in the air force, he got to see a lot of the world, but my mom never had the chance to travel much, so this was going to be the trip of a lifetime for both of them.

In February, they traveled to London, Germany, Switzerland, Austria, and finally Paris. By the time they got to Paris, my father was sick with pneumonia. He was so sick, in fact, that they felt they needed to see a doctor in Paris before flying home. The doctor advised them not to travel until my father was well. But my dad was exhausted and just wanted to go home. They flew home the next day. He had a very high fever and felt miserable. It was a horrible eight-hour flight, especially since he was so sick. But he got home and saw his doctor who gave him some antibiotics that helped him for a while.

That year, Avalon had a special event over Father's Day weekend that just happened to be near Tampa and near my parents.

I knew I would only have a short time to make a side trip, so I rented a Jaguar, drove to my parents' house, and surprised my father. I took him and my mother to lunch to celebrate Father's Day before I had to be at the concert that evening.

My parents came to the concert that night and afterward took me back to the hotel. As I got out of the car and hugged them both goodbye, my father looked at me and said, "Thank you for surprising me today, buddy. You made my day! Your mother and I are very proud of you and love you so much, son."

That September, I was in Atlanta, Georgia, with Avalon doing an outdoor concert. For some reason, we flew from Nashville to Atlanta for that event instead of driving the four hours. When we landed, I called home to check in with Stephanie. "Have you talked to your mom or dad?" she asked. "I think you should call home. Your dad isn't feeling well."

I hung up and immediately called my parents. My mother answered, and I asked her what was going on. She said, "I think your dad wants to talk to you. He's not feeling well. We think maybe he's had a reaction to his medication, so we're going to take him to the ER to get checked. But he wants to talk to you." She passed the phone to him and in a slurred tone, he said, "Hey, bud. What are you doing?"

"Well, we're on our way to a concert, Dad. Are you okay?"

"Yeah, I'm fine. I don't feel great, but I'm okay."

I told him I loved him.

"I love you, too, buddy. So much."

I reminded him to have Mom call me once they got to the doctor to let me know what was going on. He gave the phone back to my mom, and she said she would call me as soon as she knew something. Then we hung up.

That was the last time I would ever speak to my father.

* * *

The concert in Atlanta was a large outdoor event, and the weather was perfect. The crowd was huge and enthusiastic, but I just couldn't focus. I had this pit in my stomach the entire time, worrying about my father. I knew deep down that something wasn't right. The minute I walked off the stage, I called my mother.

"They're still running tests, but your father has become unresponsive. They don't know why."

I immediately told her I was coming home.

"Don't come home yet, Jody. He's going to be okay. The doctors don't think there's anything to worry about. Just go on back to Nashville, and I will let you know if anything changes."

My mom and dad still lived in Riverview, Florida, a suburb of Tampa, where they'd both lived for most of their married lives. When Avalon got back to the Atlanta airport to fly home, I was going to try to fly to Tampa, but Delta Airlines wouldn't change my ticket, so I was forced to fly back to Nashville. Once I got home, I told Stephanie, "Dad's not doing well, but they don't want me to come home yet, so I'm just going to play it by ear."

We didn't hear much from my mom that night, only that they were running tests and that Dad was still unresponsive. She told us to get some rest, and she would follow up with us in the morning.

Stephanie tried to comfort me as best she could that night as my stomach churned. As I laid my head down on the pillow, I thought, *Surely God won't take my dad from me this early. God knows just how important that man is to me. There's just no way He would do that to me. Not now. It's too soon.*

The phone rang around 3:00 a.m. I immediately knew before I answered it that it was bad. Why do all the bad phone calls seem to come at 3:00 a.m.? It was my brother Jim. He is typically a calm, level-headed person, but I could hear the concern and crack in his voice the moment he started to speak. "Hey, bro. So it doesn't look good. I think if you can, you need to get home ASAP. I'm getting on a flight in two hours from Philly and will meet you there." I told him I would take the first flight out that I could get.

I hung up the phone and called American Airlines. They were very kind and gave me a discounted fare. I bought an open-ended ticket to Tampa and was on the 5:45 a.m. flight. I sat in the window seat with a pit in my stomach, watching the sun come up through the clouds. I knew this wasn't going to be good. I had to connect in Dallas, of course, but by the time I arrived in Tampa, my brother was waiting for me at the airport. He had arrived about 10 minutes before me.

We drove together to Tampa General Hospital in silence. I think both of us were on the same page, not believing what was unfolding and trying to push down the fear of what we might be about to face.

When we arrived, my father hadn't regained consciousness, and the doctors couldn't figure out what was going on. The best they could tell from the barrage of tests they had run was that "there was a vegetation that had grown in his body that had broken off, and a portion of it had gone to his brain and put him in this unconscious state." His heart was weak and not working properly. Systems throughout his body were beginning to fail.

The lead cardiac doctor was Dr. Betzu, a friend of our family. His wife, Natalie, was one of my brother's closest friends when they were growing up. She and her twin sister, Nanette, and their other sister, Hope, were part of a singing trio that traveled around from time to time. Natalie and I sang together when we were younger or when I came into town for solo concerts, and Hope and I had sung together in high school. Since we were close friends with the doctor, they let us have access that we probably shouldn't have had to our dad in the critical care unit (CCU).

Looking back on it now, I better understand why hospitals impose restrictions on families being allowed in CCU. The procedures they need to perform to keep someone alive are difficult to watch, especially when it's being done to someone you care deeply about.

We spent the next 12 hours checking on him and sitting around his bed. He was hooked up to what seemed like a dozen machines. Once we realized the severity of his condition, Stephanie and her mother flew in from Nashville to be with us.

While I was despondent, Stephanie was strong. She sat by his bed and talked to him, held his hand, prayed over him, and told him he was a fighter and that he had to survive so he could see his grandchildren. She really was quite amazing, and I was useless. I sat and watched her care for and love on my father, and all I could do was stand against the wall in a catatonic state, barely able to make full sentences.

I stood there staring at this man who for my entire life had been larger than life itself. Now he looked so small and weak. It felt like God was playing the cruelest joke on me. I couldn't wrap my mind or heart around the thought of him never getting up from that bed. Yet I knew deep down that he wouldn't. God was going to take him no matter how hard we prayed. I had never experienced such certainty on what was about to happen in my life.

Dad's potassium levels kept dropping, and each time they did, he flatlined. An alarm sounded, and crews came rushing in. That happened every couple of hours. Once they resuscitated him and gave him more potassium, he got back into a normal rhythm and was fine until he used up what they had given him. Then it would happen again.

The final time they resuscitated him, it was very dramatic. His body was refusing to respond the way it had the times before. The doctor literally crawled up on top of him to give him chest compressions because his heart had stopped beating. I wish I had never seen that because those mental pictures are what I still see in my head to this day. The doctors were able to bring him back one more time, and though his pulse was very weak, he maintained for a bit on his own after they gave him more drugs and potassium.

When Dr. Betzu crawled off my dad, he looked exhausted. We were all gathered around the area, and he turned to Mom who was standing next to Richard, my oldest brother. The doctor said, "Listen, Yolie, I can keep doing this all day and all night, and I love Sonny, you know that, so I will if you want me to, but it's just going to have the same effect. He will continue to keep coding because his body is not sustaining life on its own anymore." He paused and then said, "I will do whatever you want, but you have to make a decision because we are only prolonging the inevitable."

It was then that I fell apart. My father and I were so close, but I couldn't bring myself to touch him. I couldn't get close to him. I was terrified that he was leaving me. My brothers and I stood next to my mother, who seemed to be in shock. It had all happened so quickly, even for her, and none of us expected to be in this place having to make this decision. I said out loud, "How in the world do we make that decision?"

We didn't want him to suffer. While the doctor reassured us that Dad wasn't aware of what was going on, he also told us that by this point, he had been out for so long that there would be some irreparable brain damage, and he would not have the quality of life anymore that he knew my dad would want. His quality of life had already sunk very low, and the physical abuse he was taking just by being kept alive was beyond what his poor body could handle.

Understanding where we were and what it meant, my mom, my brothers, and I decided it was time to take him off life support and sign the do not resuscitate paperwork.

Within an hour or so, he passed away. I immediately walked straight out of his room to the elevator, down to the lobby, and out the front door. Tampa General Hospital sits on the northernmost tip of Davis Island in Tampa Bay. Near the hospital is a four-and-a-half-mile strip of sidewalk along what is called Bayshore Boulevard. I crossed the bridge to the sidewalk and started to walk.

I don't even know why I took that walk except I didn't want to be anywhere near that hospital. I just needed to breathe. I felt like I was suffocating. There was a cinder block of ache in my heart, and through the sobs I could barely see where I was walking.

I reached a small, cutout area of the walk where there was a bench to sit on and look out over the bay. I leaned over the railing and felt the wind hit my face. I sensed my dad in that wind. I don't know how to explain it, but as that breeze moved around me, I could almost smell my father. It was like he had come to me—to say goodbye.

The days that followed were surreal. I witnessed the world through a foggy filter like on my wedding day, but this time, my heart was wrecked. It wasn't that I didn't understand the nature of death—that it's the natural course of life. I get it. We bury our parents. It's supposed to be that way. But he was 56 years old. He was so young and had so much more to offer. The thought of him not being there and not being able to speak into my life, my marriage, or my family anymore, the pain of knowing he would never know his grandchildren was seriously more than I was equipped to handle at that time.

My father's memorial service was simple but significant. There were hundreds of people there. Many of them at one time or another had been part of his youth group. Avalon sang several of his favorite songs, and somehow I managed to get through all of them without shedding a tear. However, the moment we were finished and I sat down next to my wife, the floodgates opened and wouldn't stop. Navigating through my grief was a process, and I was failing at it.

Avalon was finishing up their next record, *Oxygen*, and we were getting close to releasing our Christmas record. I stayed in Riverview with my mother for two weeks, as long as I possibly could, given the demands of the touring schedule. Again, my wife was brilliant, patient, and loving. She went back to Nashville and back to work and gave me the time I needed with my mom and my family to sort through all that was left behind.

Greg Long, who is now a full-time member of Avalon, was a solo artist at the time and engaged to Janna. Later, Greg came to Avalon when Michael Passons left. Greg had just finished recording his solo project called *Now*. One of the songs on the record, "In the Waiting," was a song he had written for his own father when he'd had a heart attack and was in the hospital. The week before we got the call about my dad, we had been in the studio working on finishing our record, and Greg was mixing songs for his record at another studio. He asked us, "Hey, I've got a song I want you to hear. I just finished it. Will you guys tell me what you think?"

We all stopped what we were doing, and Greg plugged his phone into the system. We listened to "In the Waiting," and I loved the song immediately. When the song was over, I said to Greg, "This song is going to help so many people." It moved me, and I wasn't even in that place yet.

When my father passed, Greg called me and asked if there was anything he could do to help. At first I said no and thank you.

Then I remembered the song. "You know what? There is. Would you mind sending me a copy of that song you played for us?" It was before we had digital, so I don't even remember how he got me the copy, but I believe he sent it to me by FedEx.

I listened to that song 5,000 times that week. It was like God's arms wrapped around me. In fact, there is a lyric in the chorus that says, "I wanna feel your arms as they surround me." I will always be grateful to Greg for that. I don't think he will ever really know how much that song helped me through that time. It reinforces in me even now the power of music and how it can sustain people and help them heal through some of the darkest moments of their lives.

Two weeks later, I boarded a plane at Tampa International and flew to New York City to do a press junket for the Christmas record. On my flight, I looked out the window at takeoff. It was an evening flight, and the sun had already set on the horizon. As the plane broke through the clouds and leveled off at cruising altitude, the sky was an inky purple and black with just a hint of orange from the nearly invisible sun.

There was a single star in the portion of the sky I could see out my window. It was so bright, it reflected off the airplane window. While I'm certain the gentleman sitting next to me probably thought I was insane, I didn't care. I began to talk to the star. I said all the things to that star I wish I had been brave enough to say when my dad was lying in that hospital bed.

I don't know how to do this without you. I've never *not* had you. You're the person who listened to me and loved me regardless of the stupid things I had done. Now that you're gone, how do I navigate life? Who do I talk to? I don't understand why God took you so early. I mean, rapists and murderers and embezzlers and pedophiles—they're rotting in prison until they're 80 or 90 or walking the streets free on bail, and God took you, a 56-year-old, precious, godly man who had done nothing but sacrifice his life for the cause of Christ. It just makes no sense. Everyone says to be strong for Mom, to be brave, that it won't hurt forever. But all I can see is what's left behind and how none of it makes any sense without you. Pop, I miss you so much it hurts to my core. How am I going to survive this?

My dad's death destroyed me spiritually. After many years on "the couch," a broken heart and desperation planted seeds of frustration and doubt about my faith and how I viewed life in general. I never turned away from my faith entirely, but Dad's death was enough for me to seriously question God's providence. How could this have been His perfect will? The grief became greater than my trust in His plan, and my heart faltered.

I started convincing myself that God didn't care for me as much as I'd always thought. If He had, He would have never taken my father so soon. He would never have allowed me or my family to hurt the way we did. I convinced myself that I had reached my own personal quota of heartache and that God would shield me from further pain. Whether that was irrational thinking or not, it was blatantly obvious to anyone around me at the time that my process had become anything but rational. In my mind, whether it was true or not, I'd been through enough, and I became angry with God.

Unfortunately, or maybe God allowed it just to prove a point, the hits just kept on coming. The record label had a huge marketing and PR plan for *Joy*, our Christmas record, and they had hired a big-shot, A-list publicist to help with the promotion.

The publicist was just a bunch of hot air, and no one could determine what he was actually doing, yet he somehow had the ability to make it look like he was super-busy. That trip to New

York City was a waste of time and resources, and I could have and should have stayed in Florida with my family.

Back in Nashville, the grind and pressure of the road was mounting. Avalon was still trying to finish *Oxygen* and had to put the recording process on hold because of my father's death and the promotion of the Christmas record. When we finally returned to the studio, Brown had already cut the track for the song "I Don't Wanna Go." It quickly became my favorite Avalon song because it brought me great comfort and reminded me of my father and his experiences when he accepted Christ and was called into ministry. It might just have been because the introduction of the song sounded like heaven to me. It somehow made me feel closer to my father.

Oxygen ended up being one of my favorite records. There's a plaque on the wall that commemorates four number-one songs in a row from that record. We ended up with six: "Make It Last Forever," "Wonder Why," "Come and Fill My Heart," "Undeniably You," "The Glory," and, of course, "I Don't Wanna Go." Despite the commercial success of the singles on the radio, overall sales began to lag a bit from previous releases.

Our record company decided to do something unprecedented. They flew the top five reporting Christian radio stations and their morning-show crews to the city of Avalon on Catalina Island off the California coast. Sparrow flew several artists from their rosters so they could promote their projects as well. When I think back on it, I can't even imagine how much it must have cost. It was a huge undertaking and a gigantic push for the *Oxygen* release. With six number-one songs, it obviously paid off.

The Platinum Campaign, as it came to be called, was an epic event. At that time, Avalon was not a platinum-selling artist. We had already sold 500,000 records of a single release, which is considered gold, but we never had a record that crossed the one million copies mark. So the record company launched this campaign under the premise that impression would become reality (aka, fake it 'til you make it). They endeavored to make us look, sound, and appear like a platinum artist in every way, and we were responsible to pay a large part of the recoupable expenses.

While I think the campaign helped *Oxygen*, several personnel changes and more time between releases resulted in a waning interest in Avalon, and the sound of CCM radio was changing. Radio wasn't as quick to add our songs to their playlists. They started pushing back harder when songs were submitted to them, saying things like, "Our listeners are looking for something fresh" or "Avalon has had their time, and we need to make room for newer, more contemporary sounds."

This was also when iTunes was being introduced into the musical landscape, and it was changing the industry in ways no one, especially those in CCM, was prepared for. No matter how difficult the process became, the record label still put pressure on us as a group to perform and deliver.

The label decided it was time to release a greatest hits compilation. There is an unspoken understanding within the music industry that when an artist releases an album of their greatest hits, their career is winding down. When they asked us to do this, knowing full well that they would do it anyway whether we wanted to or not, we all had mixed emotions. We were already struggling to get radio stations to play our music. What kind of signal would a greatest hits record send?

A few months after the release of *Oxygen*, our soprano, Cherie Adams, decided she wanted to move on, be a mother and a wife, and take a different path. That's when Melissa Green stepped in. She and I had known each other for years. She was also a TRUTH alumnus and had strong, soprano chops. Just before we began production on the three additional singles we would include on the greatest hits collection, Melissa came on board to be part of Avalon.

We released *The Very Best of Avalon, Testify to Love* on March 25, 2003. The collection had three new songs, and two of them—"Everything to Me" and "New Day"—went to number one. Those would be the last two singles to make it to the number one spot in Christian radio for a long time.

We also won an American Music Award (AMA) that year for Inspirational Artist of the Year. We were up against P.O.D. and Jars of Clay for the honor. We were the only artists to show up, and many CCM publicists speculated that was the only reason we won the award. It felt like even our own industry no longer wanted us to succeed, and while winning the AMA was definitely a highlight, there was a skeptical undertone: "Did we really deserve this award, or did the AMAs just give it to us to save face on national television?"

We released four more records between 2004 and 2006, constantly trying to find something that would appeal to radio while being pushed by management and the record company to try to reinvent ourselves so we could regain some of the earlier success we had been blessed with.

It seemed like no matter how hard we tried, we always came up short. With each year and project that passed and each professional failure, I began to isolate myself more and more.

Avalon was rapidly moving from being a cutting-edge pop group to becoming an inspirational artist. Christian music was undergoing massive changes. Artists like TobyMac were coming on the scene, and a more progressive, rock sound was starting to gain wider acceptance. Christian rap and R&B started taking off, creating its own genre. We were slowly being diluted. The trends were shifting. I think we were all starting to realize that maybe we just needed to be grateful for what we had accomplished and move on.

Time and perspective helped me recognize that we were just part of the machine. Grant Cunningham had passed away, and Avalon was passed off to a new artist representation at the label, which changed the entire group dynamic. Grant had a lot of responsibility for the sound of Avalon and was a great advocate for us. If we didn't have a song that worked for the sound of Avalon, Grant wrote one. He played a key part in our success, so when he passed away, it was a huge knock in the gut for us in a million ways.

The new A&R (artists and repertoire) person didn't have the same vested interest in us that Grant had. Nothing against him personally, but he cared because he was being paid to care. He also had a whole other roster of artists to worry about, and he had brought some of them to the table.

The pressure to maintain something that was not maintainable anymore began to eat away at all of us. Brown Bannister was not producing our records anymore; he had moved on to other things, probably due in large part to our sales slowing down and, with that, our recording budgets. He had other new opportunities he wanted to pursue. The record company couldn't justify spending the money to hire a producer like Brown anymore.

They decided to move us to a new producer who was extremely talented but felt forced to change our sound even more in order to motivate radio and sales.

It didn't work.

THIRTEEN:
THE UNRAVELING

In the midst of what were some of the most challenging times for Avalon, something miraculous happened. Stephanie and I found out we were pregnant.

Both of us had struggled because we thought we wouldn't be able to have children, but in the fall of 2004, we found out we were having a baby girl. Sarah-Clayton was born in March 2005, and she has been a source of sheer joy and laughter in our home ever since. She has her mother's wit and beauty and her father's musical sense and gift of sarcasm (the latter makes me the proudest).

While my heart was completely overwhelmed with love for my new daughter, it was also reeling from the fact that my father would never be able to know how incredible his granddaughter is, at least not on this side of heaven. Nor would Sarah-Clayton be able to understand just how precious her pop-pop was.

I tell people often that of all the things I've had to work through in my life, my father's death will always be my greatest human heartache. I say "human" because I know our trials are temporary, and my daughter will spend eternity with her pop-pop in heaven. But for now, here in our earthly home, I wish more than almost anything that they knew each other.

Being a new father, while obviously incredible, only added to the stress I already felt about needing to be home more often. Avalon was having to work just as hard, if not harder, for less money to keep up with our budget obligations. The stress of a waning career and the pressure Avalon was feeling from all sides to continue to deliver was more emotionally and physically crushing for me than I realized.

Stephanie was working as a creative director at Provident Music, the CCM arm of Sony Music. She moved up in the ranks and was in charge of all imaging and packaging for releases. That meant she started traveling as well. We took Sarah-Clayton to Stephanie's parents while we passed like two ships in the night. We seldom saw each other, and that began to put even more strain on an already strained relationship.

There was an emotional stress that was building inside of me that I couldn't control. My heart was growing cold and indifferent to everything and everyone. I would sit in the corner of the bus after concerts, put my headphones on, and watch movies on my laptop. I wouldn't engage with anyone. I didn't want to be there anymore.

I started to develop extremely unhealthy relationships with people, and what's even worse, I took advice from those who weren't qualified to speak into my life in the first place. As I look back on it now, I am baffled by my own ignorance. I was letting people whose lives were far more dysfunctional than mine speak into my life, and I was listening to them. I was looking everywhere I could to distract myself from the ever-growing pressure within me and around me.

For a short while, I found some distractions and a group of people who were willing to entertain those distractions. What's even sadder is that those people probably looked to me as a spiritual leader because of both my career status with Avalon and the fact that I was a Christian, and I let them down greatly. I was far from being anyone's spiritual leader, especially then. The disappointment in myself fills me with sadness even to this day.

Beyond the behavioral and mental dysfunction, I was also developing a physical reaction to the stress. I started not feeling well. That's vague, I know, but the only way I can describe it is that I could just tell something wasn't right. I started to get dizzy when I sang or exercised. I attributed it to stress and that I had gained some weight. I thought I was just out of shape.

I had moments during a concert when I had to step to the side because I couldn't catch my breath. One night when we were in Ohio doing a Christmas concert, I became so dizzy and nauseous after a difficult solo that I nearly passed out.

When I told Stephanie about it, she begged me to make an appointment for a checkup. Because we had spent so little time together, we were planning an anniversary trip, but she wanted me to see a doctor before we left. At the doctor's office, they ran a battery of tests on me since the symptoms could have been a sign of any number of health issues.

When Stephanie and I left for our trip, we were still waiting on the results and a final diagnosis from the doctor. Since my doctor was a family friend, he said he would contact me on our trip and let me know what he found out.

The blood work came back inconclusive but with obvious markers that indicated a problem. The doctor called me and said he wanted me to see a cardiologist right away. The moment we returned from our trip, he fast-tracked me to a doctor he preferred at St. Thomas Heart in Nashville.

After another series of tests and blood work, the doctor diagnosed me with hypertrophic cardiomyopathy. The doctor said it's known as the silent killer because all too often, people don't realize they have it and overexert themselves, causing heart failure. We often hear stories of athletes out on the field playing football, on the court playing basketball, or running the track who just drop. Most of them do not survive because they have a hypertrophism or enlarged heart. Because they were otherwise in such excellent physical condition, they exhibited little or no symptoms and didn't know until it was too late. While I wasn't in horrible shape at the time, the fact that I had let myself go a little might have been what saved me.

The doctor also discovered that I had a genetic abnormality with my heart muscle where the muscle atrophies over time. By then, I had lost 19 percent of my heart muscle function, which explained my shortness of breath and the inability to sustain a normal, daily routine without feeling overly fatigued.

I have to admit that I drove home from the doctor that day feeling like this was my just penance for the poor choices I had made. The darkness that had been lurking for so long started to close in on me, and the depths of my depression, which I didn't realize I was in at the time, started planting a death wish within my soul. If not consciously then subconsciously, I was losing the will to fight, and this new diagnosis only sealed that deal. I had zero emotional or spiritual accountability and felt I had nowhere to turn for relief.

Make no mistake, the voices pushing for success were still coming at me from all sides. Management, record label, the expectation was still there, but this diagnosis of heart disease would prove to be the final straw. It wouldn't be long before I would hit that brick wall. All that darkness and carelessness would bury me under the rubble as the pieces of my life would finally come crumbling down around me.

My marriage was dissolving quickly, not for any reason other than the poor choices I was making. Stephanie and I separated for several days and struggled knowing how to put our family back together. She told me, "You have to choose now what you want because I'm just about done, and if you want this to work, it's going to take some major changes on your end."

She was so hurt and devastated by who I had become, and she was right to be. I wasn't even sure who I was anymore. She had been as patient and gracious as anyone could have ever been given the situation, and I was actually surprised that she even had an ounce of fight left in her.

While we were separated, I was at my brother's home in Philadelphia. While I was there, I woke up once in the middle of the night sweating and went to the bathroom. I turned on the light and splashed cold water on my face because I was so hot and couldn't get comfortable. When I looked at myself in the mirror, someone I didn't recognize was looking back at me. It wasn't my face. It was someone darker, older, more sinister-looking, almost demonic. It terrified me so much that I nearly passed out in that small bathroom.

The next morning, I wondered if it had been a nightmare, but I knew deep down that it wasn't. It was my reflection looking back at me. That was who I had become. I believe God gave me a glimpse of what I looked like from the inside out, and it terrified me to my core.

I decided the time had come to step away from Avalon and travel for a while. I recommitted to my wife and family that we would work through the obstacles I had created for us. I was in it with them forever, and I would do whatever it took to save my marriage, to save my family. At the time, I truly believed I had hit rock bottom. Little did I know I had further still to fall.

I called Janna and told her, "I'm not coming back."

∗ ∗ ∗

I came home and started putting the broken pieces of my family and my health back together. Because I was no longer employed, finding a source of income was at the top of my list. My wife's family owns a merchandising company, and they hired me even though I was highly unqualified and really had no clue what I was doing. Apart from my time at Liberty, I never felt more out of place.

When I started at USimprints, my father-in-law asked me how much I had made every two weeks with Avalon. When I told him, a look of shock came over his face. He asked me if I was kidding. "How have you survived?" he said. I let him know it was thanks to Stephanie's job, a strict budget, and a consistent paycheck. When he hired me, he said, "I'm going to do better than that," and he doubled my pay. He paid me far more than I deserved since I had no experience in this field.

I learned quickly and tried to work hard. I was actually one of the top two or three sales reps every week out of a group of 10. But nepotism had definite side effects. Other employees resented me for working there. They ran to my father-in-law or brother-in-law who shared the leadership responsibilities and complained about what I did or didn't do. The people responsible for payroll complained about what I was being paid. Mistakes were tolerated unless they were made by me, and then there was hell to pay. Tempers flared, and the atmosphere often became volatile. It was an unhealthy environment, and it ended up adding more fuel to my dysfunctional fire, which I was not able to handle either mentally or spiritually.

Eventually, the backlash from my employment there became too much for my brother-in-law. He devised a plan that would set me up in a remote office on the other side of town with a small staff. I showed up every day with no clue what I was supposed to do. The phone stopped ringing. The sales stopped coming in. I served no purpose at all.

Eventually, my brother-in-law told me he couldn't afford to pay me anymore and had to let me go. I suppose it was inevitable, but that didn't make it sting any less. He let me go in July and paid me until September. After that, I was on my own with no consistent income. My time there lasted five and a half years.

On the day he fired me, I stood in the restroom at this little satellite office and looked in the mirror and wept. *I deserve this,* I thought. *I'm useless. I'm damaged goods, and I serve no real purpose anymore.* Remember, I grew up Baptist where you followed the letter of the law or you suffered the consequences of your backslidden ways. I was convinced that I was reaping what I had sown. God was obviously choosing to use all the other "perfect" people, and I was done.

I know, I know, once again it sounds like one big pity party, and you would be right. It was. But this was just one more straw being piled on the proverbial camel's back.

On a positive note (I'm sure you could use one at this point), during this season off the road, Stephanie and I reconciled and were working on our marriage. Every marriage has peaks and valleys. I'm thankful that while in the valley, she continued to walk with me instead of running from me. We were finally getting to the peak again, and I'm so glad we both decided to stay.

Marriage is difficult, beautiful, frustrating, and inspiring. It is truly life personified in a relationship. But marriage is always worth fighting for. People often give up too quickly, trading one set of problems for another relationship with a different set of problems. When you are able to persevere and come through great difficulty, you not only fall in love with your spouse all over again but you create a bond with them that no one can break. I'm truly thankful that we worked so hard to get our relationship back on track. We had to grow and learn to be strong for one another because we were about to fight another battle on a different front that neither of us saw coming.

A friend of ours invited us to a wedding in Hickman County, Tennessee. I described it as a redneck wedding, but in Hickman County, what other type of wedding is there? For some reason, I didn't go, so my wife and my brother attended without me.

The day after the wedding, my wife and I were getting our bathing suits on to get in the pool, and she asked me to look at a mark underneath her right breast. I realized the mark was actually a tick that had burrowed into her skin. She freaked out and started screaming, "Get it out! Get it out!" By the time I pulled it out, it had made a bull's-eye imprint on her skin. We put some topical antiseptic on it and went to the pool.

We didn't think anything of it, but within a couple of weeks, Stephanie was the sickest I'd ever seen anybody in my life. I've been around cancer patients and people struggling with AIDS, but I have never seen anyone immobilized and crippled by something so quickly. She lay on the couch, moaning in pain, every joint in her body throbbing. She could barely move, and her mind was foggy. She struggled to put her thoughts into words.

This continued on and off for months, and as it did, the symptoms got worse. We went to several doctors looking for answers.

Each one prescribed pain medication or steroids, but no one could pinpoint the cause. One doctor went so far as to say Stephanie was mentally unstable and needed an intervention. I wanted to come across the table at his smug, arrogant attitude, but I restrained myself. Obviously, if he couldn't diagnose the problem, there must not be one. Interestingly, that doctor is no longer practicing medicine. The next doctor we went to said she was having a mental breakdown, to which she replied, "Yeah, I'm having a mental breakdown! It's because I'm sick, and I need somebody to help me."

I finally realized what the word *practicing* medicine really meant because a lot of these doctors were still practicing. We ate through every bit of our savings, and the doctor bills were piling up. That was during the time when the Affordable Care Act—aka Obamacare—was put into law, and our health insurance changed drastically. We had giant deductibles we could never meet regardless of how much we were charged. We were responsible for every penny, and even though it was financially astronomical, I would have paid with my own life to heal my wife.

For more than a year, we struggled to find a doctor who could help us figure out what was wrong with Stephanie. She was so sick that all she did was lie on the couch with every joint in her body throbbing in pain. Our daughter, who was five at the time, came up to her and said, "Mommy, come play with me." Stephanie just cried and told her she couldn't. It broke my heart. These symptoms weren't in her head. She was in real pain, and I felt helpless.

After seeing eight doctors, we finally found a neurologist who was patient and determined to find the answer. She ran just about every test she could think of, and they all came back negative, which you would think would be a relief to us. But those negative results made us upset because we were desperate for an answer— any answer.

We went in for a consultation and to review the results of the many tests the neurologist had run. She looked at us and said, "I don't know what else to try. Everything comes back normal." We said we understood and told her we were grateful for her thoroughness and how kind she had been. She was about to say goodbye when a thought occurred to her. She asked, "You haven't by any chance been bitten by a tick, have you?" We told her that she had. "Stephanie, you may have Lyme's disease."

The doctor took Stephanie's blood one more time and had it tested for the disease. Sure enough, one week later, the results came back not only positive but practically off the charts. It was confirmed; she suffered from Lyme's disease.

That diagnosis began yet another journey of doctors who had no clue how to treat the disease or argued that the disease didn't exist in the state of Tennessee. It was 2009, and at that time, we got pushback everywhere we turned from the medical community regarding treatment. They put Stephanie on heavy antibiotics that had no effect on the disease but destroyed her digestive system. She was almost *more* miserable, if that was even possible.

One day, we were speaking to a musician friend of ours about all that was going on, and he and his wife mentioned a doctor in Atlanta who had helped some patients with Lyme's disease get some relief. They warned us that he was a holistic doctor and the cost probably wouldn't be covered under our insurance. That gave us a good laugh and we said, "What's insurance?"

I had no idea what holistic medicine was. Stephanie had heard of it but decided to read up on it. I was being treated for my heart from a traditional, Western-medicine doctor, so I didn't see the point in Eastern medicine. It seemed like a bunch of hocus-pocus to me. I was skeptical, and it was very expensive. I had this mindset: "If you're sick, you just take a pill." But Stephanie asked if we could please try it. I would have done anything for Stephanie, so I agreed.

With the help of our friends, we were able to get in with the Atlanta doctor, and in May, we went to see him. Dr. Anderson was a kind man, a hippie who had radically accepted Christ in the '60s. I liked him well enough, but the entire experience was just weird for me. I had been managing my heart condition for a few years, and his approach ran contrary to what I was used to.

However, by the time we left, he had confirmed she had Lyme's disease and had given her a treatment plan to proceed on the path to healing. After hearing "no" and "I don't know" for so long, we now actually had a plan. It was an emotional moment during our visit when Dr. Anderson grabbed her hand, looked her in the eyes, and said, "You're not going to die from this. You're going to be okay, and together we're going to get you well." We both broke down and could barely console ourselves. It was like we had been fumbling around in a dark room for so long and finally someone had turned on the light.

The treatment plan was not for the fainthearted. It involved several months of detox and discipline, and there were moments when I think Stephanie felt like the cure was worse than the disease. But the cure did happen. By December of that year, Dr. Anderson was able to give Stephanie the best Christmas gift she'd ever received—a Lyme's-free diagnosis.

Since making Stephanie's story public, I've had hundreds of people share their stories with me about loved ones or friends who struggle with Lyme's. They want to know what we did because in many cases, like us, they'd been trying remedies for years and nothing helped. I've sent countless people to Dr. Anderson and Longevity Health Care in Roswell, Georgia. I don't get any kind of kickback from them. I just don't want people to struggle or suffer anymore. There is a cure.

I'm not anti-Western medicine because that and God's grace have kept me alive. When I was diagnosed with my heart condition, I struggled to find medication that worked for me that didn't also have strong side effects. Once we found the proper balance, my cardiologist made a somewhat radical suggestion to me. He recommended that I take part in a clinical trial that was being supported at Vanderbilt University Medical Center. The process would involve using stem cells to reanimate dead heart muscle tissue. He felt it could have positive results for me. I agreed and signed on to participate in the trial.

The treatment made me so sick for the first two months that I could barely get out of bed. I've never had chemotherapy, but I've had people tell me that the symptoms I described were similar to a chemo treatment. By the time the trial was over, I had had nearly a year of treatment. The test results didn't show any significant change in my atrophied heart muscle tissue. It was disappointing to say the least.

When I started the clinical trial, I was at 36 percent heart muscle loss. When it ended, my measurement was around 34 percent. The doctors didn't think the improvement was enough to be considered a success. The good news is that my heart muscle loss stopped at 34 percent. It's been at that level for nearly 15 years, which has given me the opportunity to adapt to it and learn how to live with it. My doctor feels very strongly that the clinical trial is responsible for why my muscle deterioration stopped increasing.

I was so disappointed when I found out the clinical trial hadn't worked. I had placed a lot of hope in the prospect of that trial, praying it would reverse some of the damage to my heart. I wasn't aware that my numbers had stopped; I was only aware that the trial hadn't worked. Subconsciously, that failed attempt got filed away with all the other failures, setbacks, and mistakes of my past. That file, full of emotional, physical, and spiritual trauma, was starting to overflow, and because I was forcing myself to be an overcomer and a survivor, I just shut it all out and pressed on. I assumed that if I pretended like none of it mattered, it wouldn't.

I would soon find out that I was wrong.

FOURTEEN:
THE AWAKENING

I sat at a table that afternoon outside the coffee shop that was directly below my remote office. I had just been let go from my job. I thought about whether or not I should go in for a coffee, whether or not I could afford a $6 cup of joe since I was now officially in the land of the unemployed. The traffic, both pedestrian and vehicular on that particular corner of Franklin called Five Points, was always bustling. This day was no exception. There were tables to the left and right of me, each one with different conversations but just loud enough so I could hear them over the road noise.

At the table to my left were three guys, all much younger than I was and definitely of the hipster variety given their lingo and affection for the fedora. They were discussing a writing gig they had just left and how partnering with the other writers had been a complete waste of their precious time. At the table to my right was a moderately well-known CCM artist and what looked like a manager or road manager–type person. She was discussing, surprisingly loudly, how frustrated she was that her last single only made it to number six on the charts.

I listened to them both as I pretended to stare down at my cell phone. My heart was filled with jealousy and frustration. I thought, *If you guys only knew how fleeting all of this is and how lucky you guys are to be in the thick of it. I'll never have that chance again.* The pit in my stomach grew as I listened and tried to figure out what my next steps would be.

Stephanie had quit her job to stay home and take care of our daughter. Several people had called to ask if I would be interested in singing, but I turned them down because I believed I wasn't good enough anymore. I was convinced that my time had passed, and it was now someone else's season. God didn't want to use me; I was damaged goods.

Several days later, I was outside mowing the front lawn when I got a phone call from Roger Breland. JRB was always like that. You wouldn't hear from him for months, maybe even years, and then he'd just call out of the blue and ask you to take his trash out. It's one of the many funny yet quirky traits that I love about him.

It was a Wednesday morning when I saw his name pop up on my phone. I had barely said hello when he asked, "Can you be in Africa by Friday?" I laughed out the words, "No! That's not even physically possible, is it?" But it turns out that yes, it is.

Roger was on the board of directors for Benny Hinn, the well-known faith healer and evangelist. Roger told me that Benny's ministry was going to be in Uganda and needed someone to come and sing special music. I told him it was just too far and not enough notice and that I didn't think I could make it work. He told me they were offering to pay me $10,000 plus travel and lodging if I would come.

I landed in Uganda on Friday morning, exhausted and nervous. I really had no idea what to expect, and JRB had only given me small bits of information about what it would be like. I had heard many stories about Benny Hinn, and being from a Southern Baptist background, I was more than a little terrified of the whole thing.

Someone from the local promoter's office picked me up at the airport and drove me to the hotel. On our way, we passed some of the worst poverty I had ever seen. People were bathing in the streets and living in cardboard boxes. It was shocking.

I noticed we were passing by an extremely long wall. It was at least 20 feet high and seemed to be surrounding a compound of some sort. We made a left turn and pulled up to a gatehouse where guards with machine guns patrolled the entrance to the compound. The sign ahead of us read, "Welcome to the Kampala Serena Hotel."

We drove through the gates and entered what looked like a completely different world. Gardens and fountains dotted the property; people dressed in white tended the grounds. Up ahead I could see the main resort complex with its majestic entrance and waterfalls flowing directly under the main lobby. It made me feel uncomfortable to realize that on the other side of that wall was the worst poverty I had ever seen. I was also uncomfortable that no one from Benny Hinn Ministries (BHM) was there to greet me. I had zero idea what to do or where to go.

I checked into the hotel, and someone escorted me to my massive hotel room, complete with private butler access. I collapsed on the bed, exhausted from the trip. I was awakened by a phone call from the BHM tour manager. He welcomed me and told me to meet him in the lobby at 5:00, dressed in a full suit and tie. I thought, *It's only 103 degrees outside. I'm sure that will be comfy.*

We took a small bus to a soccer arena on the outskirts of Kampala. When we arrived, nearly three hours before the event was scheduled to start, there were already thousands of people there—waiting.

Before we started, someone told me I would sing two to three songs, and JRB told me to bring several of my backing tracks to give them options to choose from. They didn't really seem thrilled with any of my songs. In fact, musically speaking, they hadn't heard of any Avalon songs, nor did they seem interested in my singing them. I did happen to have the track to Greg Long's song "Mercy Said No." To this day, I still don't think they had ever heard of it but just thought the title seemed nice.

Once the service started, I ended up singing that one and only song for the nearly four-hour event. We went back to the hotel afterward, and I went to bed. The next day, I boarded a plane for home. On the entire flight home, I thought, *What just happened? What in the world did I just fly halfway around the world for? It hasn't even been 48 hours!* I was just baffled by it all.

The experience of being at one of Benny Hinn's crusades was a little traumatic in and of itself, especially for this more conservative Baptist kid from down South. There was so much I didn't understand or just wasn't used to, like people falling on the floor as though someone had pushed them over or the way Benny had so many handlers and security like he was the president of the United States or a prime minister or something. And why had I flown all the way to Africa just to sing one song, a song that I suppose was worth $10,000. Even though we desperately needed the money, it all just seemed so odd to me.

The lack of organization and communication, the grandstanding and theatrics—I came home and thought, *Whew! I'm glad that's over. I'll never do that again.* It took BHM nearly four months to pay what they owed me, but I eventually did receive the money.

Pastor Benny Hinn (PBH) must have liked something about my performance because he had his people reach out to me and ask me to come back. This time, it was for a bit less money than before, but it was still substantial enough to lure this unemployed musician. I ended up doing a couple more dates with the ministry. This time, the event was in Surabaya, Indonesia.

I arrived a couple days before the rest of the ministry personnel. Several of the main entourage had been delayed along with Pastor Benny. Once several of them arrived, we learned that PBH would not be coming. He pulled out of the trip at the last minute because he was working through his divorce and didn't feel up to the long trip. The event went on for three nights, and I sang quite a bit more to help compensate for the fact that he wasn't there.

I made a couple more trips with them, and then things went silent for a while, most likely because PBH was working through some difficulties in his private life. After several months, I received another phone call to see if I would be interested in coming back to Indonesia with BHM so Benny could make up for his absence. I agreed, and we all met again in Surabaya almost a year later.

Needless to say, if you've ever flown anywhere in Asia, it is a very long and exhausting trip. I was still getting used to my heart condition—learning to pace myself and figuring out my limits. Greg Wiggins, one of my friends from my time in TRUTH, was BHM's full-time piano player. When I walked into a restaurant in Surabaya after that long flight, I was so relieved to see a familiar and welcoming face, something you didn't see a lot when on the road with BHM.

Greg and I spent the first afternoon in Surabaya getting caught up and laughing about old TRUTH and JRB stories. It had been years since we had spoken, and obviously a lot had transpired in both of our lives. At that time, I was traveling with a nitroglycerine tablet in my pocket in case I had a heart episode. I never really spoke about it to anyone because it all seemed so dramatic and, quite honestly, extreme. But for some reason, I told Greg about the nitro and how I always carried it in my pocket, just in case. I told him, "If I ever go down, be sure to give me this tablet as soon as possible." Always the practical joker, I was surprised at how very seriously he took this information, and I was grateful to have someone I could count on to be there with me.

By now, I had gotten used to the more charismatic style of PBH's services and started to challenge myself to try to be more open-minded about who God was and what He was truly capable of. That night at the service, there was an unusually powerful movement of God like I had never seen before. If you've ever seen a Benny Hinn crusade, I'm sure you've seen what I talked about earlier—people falling or being slain in the Spirit. It was something I had always been a bit skeptical of. But the more I was out with BHM, the more I witnessed the power of God and felt His presence in a real way, and the more I realized that God can do whatever He wants with people. And who was I to judge whether or not something was authentic? Regardless of how I felt, many people fell that night. In fact, at one point I was trapped in the middle of the stage, surrounded by bodies. I just kept singing.

When the event ended, we went backstage to a large area where we would have dinner and meet the local pastors. There was a separate, more private, glassed-in area where the VIP guests usually sat. Since PBH had already gone back to the hotel and wasn't there, we were free to use that room, so I went inside and sat on a couch.

A husband and wife came in and asked if they could join me. They had been on the BHM staff for many years. Sheryl played the organ for PBH. She was a funny, down-to-earth, loving woman who had a great heart of compassion for people. She had endured a lot being out with the ministry for so long. It was not an easy gig.

She and her husband began asking me about my life, and we got around to discussing my health. I told her about my heart issues and how it was a struggle to even breathe at times. They both agreed that they should immediately pray for me to be healed. I figured, *What have I got to lose?* So we stood, and they laid hands on me and began praying. The moment they began to pray, I could feel it. It was strong. I had been in several services and never felt the power of God like I did in this little glassed-in room. I felt heat surge through my body, and before I could do anything to stop it, my body went limp. I couldn't stand anymore. They caught me and continued to pray, asking God to heal my heart as I collapsed to the ground.

In the other room, Greg was finishing up his dinner, laughing with some of the other staff. At one point, he looked over and saw me on the ground with Sheryl and her husband standing over me. He dropped his plate of food and ran into the room, screaming, "It's in his pocket! In his jacket pocket!"

Everyone stopped praying, and Sheryl's husband said, "What's in his pocket?" Greg sputtered, "His nitroglycerine!" At that, I began to chuckle. Sheryl and her husband looked puzzled, and then we all began to laugh uncontrollably while Greg stared at us, panting and panicky. Once he realized what had happened, he started laughing as well and wiped his brow. He sank into one of the chairs and said, "Thank God! I thought it was the big one."

The BHM team invited me to sing with them a couple more times, and eventually, after an event in Amsterdam, they asked me to join the team full-time. The pay would be much less, on a per-day basis, but travel and lodging would be provided, and I'd also be paid for travel days. I agreed and thus began an almost four-year adventure with BHM traveling the world. Our income was lean, but I didn't have any other options, and Stephanie and I felt like it was the right move for me.

I quickly realized how drastic the change would be for our family life. This wasn't just "I'll be away from home for a few days." Most of the time, I was thousands of miles away from home on the other side of the world. Ironically, that was one of the parts of the job I loved most. When I started with Benny Hinn Ministries, my passport was practically empty with only a few stamps in it. By the time I left, it was full, and I had to add pages, which were almost full as well. I got to travel the world, make amazing friends, and see incredible places. But the most incredible thing by far was how God opened my eyes to new experiences—experiences that my Baptist upbringing did not prepare me for.

I have been exposed to all kinds of denominations and seen a lot in my years on the road. But I found myself continuously surprised and at times even shocked at what I saw while I was out with BHM. In one of my first services with them as a full-time musician on his staff, we were in Africa holding a crusade in a huge soccer arena. There were more than 10,000 people in attendance and another 250 people sitting on the platform. A large choir was also assembled behind the stage. During the healing portion of the service, PBH brought people up on the platform to testify of their healings that had taken place prior to the service starting. Sometimes they wouldn't even speak; Benny would just touch their faces, and they would fall.

This particular service was getting intense. Even PBH's handlers and staff were falling. He yelled the word *fire*, and people collapsed in waves across the arena and on the platform. It wasn't a scene I'd ever witnessed before. You may have already picked up on this trait about me, but I can be a bit cynical and sarcastic. It wasn't that I didn't believe a person could be knocked on their rear by the Holy Spirit. Heck, I had firsthand experience of the power of being prayed over from that night in Indonesia. This night, however, it felt like it was more theatrical than sincere. I certainly wasn't feeling it . . . at all.

By the time the service was drawing to a close, the stage, choir loft, and audience were littered with people who had been slain in the Spirit. Once again, I was standing in the middle of a pile of people singing "Holy, Holy, Holy Are You Lord." PBH was scurrying around the stage, and for a moment, he caught my eye and stopped and stared at me. Maybe the word *glared* would be a better word. It was only for two or three seconds, but I could feel his eyes looking me over disapprovingly.

This happened several times over the next few months—every time when the masses were falling all around me. I would be standing there surrounded by bodies and continuing to sing. Each time, PBH looked at me with that look. I could tell he was growing frustrated with me, but I have to admit that a big part of me started to wonder if people were truly feeling the power of God. I watched as people fell and then peeked out of one eye to see if anyone had noticed. I also sometimes caught BHM staffers fall and then immediately look around to see what PBH was going to do next. Were they being told to do that or just trying to get attention? The same "falling out" of sometimes entire congregations happened almost every night, probably for about six months. The more it happened and I didn't participate, the more I could tell PBH was getting annoyed.

It was common for PBH to have us come to his green room after the service and discuss the evening, even though the services weren't over until close to midnight and we were all exhausted. He told us stories, and we discussed how it seemed like people were "in the flesh" that night, meaning people were faking their healings, falling disingenuously or not falling at all. One night after the first of three nights at a North Carolina event, we came into PBH's room, and he immediately looked at me and shouted, "Why do you resist the Holy Spirit?"

I looked back at him with a bewildered expression, but I knew exactly what he was referring to. I politely but firmly told him, "I don't resist the Holy Spirit. I want this, all of this, if it is real. But you've got people on your platform who are falling for a paycheck. You've got people who are lying on the ground supposedly slain in the Spirit, and they've got one eye open making sure they don't miss what you do next. I don't want to be that person. When it happens to me, it will have to be real. I won't fall for a paycheck."

He left the room, frustrated with me, and never brought it up again. I'm not sure if it bothered him or if he respected my answer. Not many people would stand up to him that way. It probably shocked him. For the most part, especially when it came to the people who were responsible for moving him around from day to day, PBH was surrounded by yes people. They kept him sheltered, protected, and private, always telling him the positives and avoiding the negatives, and there were many negatives on any given day.

Sometimes it seemed that this sheltered, constant ego-stroking was only to his detriment. It often made him socially awkward and difficult to have a one-on-one conversation with. He and I couldn't have been more opposite. I tried to joke with him or have a normal conversation, but it was as if he didn't have time for any of it.

While I was with BHM, I became good friends with Benny's son, Josh, and his nephew William. They both had been around charismatic ministries their entire lives and seemed to be in tune with the Holy Spirit. They were willing to help me understand more of what it was all about. They weren't stuffy. They were funny and down to earth. Josh had a reputation for being a bad boy, and he was definitely capable of living up to that. However, he was kind, compassionate, fun-loving, and truly wanted nothing more than to please his father—something very difficult to do. I often felt sorry for him because it was so obvious to me how desperate he was for his father's attention and how he acted out to try to illicit a response from him. I always said that if Josh could bridle all his wild tendencies, he would be one of the most incredible pastors this world has ever known, even more so than his own father.

William was PBH's brother's son. You could see a major difference in William's family dynamic. It was obvious that his father had gone to great pains to make sure he was present in his children's lives. Their family was the complete opposite of PBH's in every way. Not only did William have a mature outlook on God, he was also more focused and disciplined than most people his age. William's father is an incredible pastor with a great heart for people and a lot of energy and fervor. William is following in his footsteps and has become a brilliant speaker in his own right.

I learned a lot about the Holy Spirit from William, and while we were on the road together, we became close friends. We laughed often, usually at my expense. However, we could also have incredibly deep conversations about wanting to go deeper into the presence of God and how I desperately needed that.

After a service in Charlotte, North Carolina, William, Josh, and I were walking back to our hotel after grabbing a bite to eat. We started talking about the Holy Spirit, and I admitted my struggle to feel the Spirit. While I didn't fully understand it at the time, I was starting to sink deeply into severe depression and anxiety. Those things were clouding my mind and heart and keeping me from focusing on anything spiritual. I felt frustrated and worried that I was in some way cut off from having those Holy Ghost experiences. Or maybe it was because I had done too many bad things to be granted access to God that way.

On top of all that mess, I was also struggling with some test results I had received prior to that trip. My physical health was faltering, and I poured out all that information to them as we walked.

It was late, and there weren't many people on the street that night, so William started praying. I'm not sure how to describe what happened that evening. All I know is that I have never before or since felt the power of God descend like He did that night. We were literally a block away from the Hyatt Hotel, and I could barely stand, let alone walk. We fell to our knees and began worshipping right there on the sidewalk, weeping and crying out to God.

After about 10 minutes of trying to move, I gave up and let the power of God take over. To say we were overwhelmed would be an understatement. I don't remember how we got back to the hotel and in our beds. I just remember waking up the next day and thinking, *Oh, wow! That's what it feels like. That's what this is all about.* For the first time in my life, I had tasted what it was like to be overwhelmed by the presence of God. And in that moment, every heartache, every disappointment, and every bit of my illness went away. I realized I wanted more.

Over the course of the next few weeks and months, I knew it was never about the falling; it was all about total surrender to God. My spirit was open to the supernatural effect of worship. There are moves of the Holy Spirit that I can't and won't understand, and that's okay. God doesn't have to consult me every time He wants to move, and it's my responsibility to just be sensitive when He does.

The first time I ever heard a person speak in tongues was at Mount Paran Central in Atlanta, Georgia, when I was younger.

The pastor was praying, and a woman from the back of the church began to speak loudly in tongues. It scared me to death because I had never heard anything like it before. As I got older, the Lord started to make my heart more pliable to His Spirit. Ephesians 3:20 (NIV) says, "Now to him who is able to do immeasurably more than all we ask or imagine, according to his power that is at work within us." Some things are real and true whether we believe them or not, and God doesn't require our faith in order to move. I'm so thankful He moves *despite* our lack of faith. If it was all based on our faith alone, we would be in big trouble.

We get so adamant about believing or not believing in something because we think it's ludicrous or it doesn't line up with our religious beliefs. Ephesians 6:12 (KJV) says, "We wrestle not against flesh and blood, but against principalities, against powers, against the rulers of the darkness of this world." There is no denying the reality of a spiritual realm. We cannot see it, and we don't fully understand it, yet the Holy Spirit does work in that realm that goes beyond anything we can comprehend. In my early years with BHM, my mind and heart slowly started to understand and accept that, and I will be forever grateful for that season of my life.

I've always been a bit of a doubting Thomas. I have to see or experience something before I actually believe it. I'm not saying that's the right way to be; I think we've already established in this book that I am not a perfect man. In my many years on the road, I have seen a lot of the theatrics that take place in church. I know I will probably get into trouble for saying this, but many in the Pentecostal Church and some in the Charismatic Movement as a whole seem to do more harm than good for the real move of the Holy Spirit. There is too much artifice and too many who crave attention that rise up in the ranks and become leaders in churches.

Obviously, I don't blame God for that. I remember what PBH used to say, that it was all just humans operating in the flesh. Even though there were many moments like that while I was on the road with BHM, there were also moments that were unmistakably God, and even Pastor Benny knew it.

A genuine move of the Spirit is palpable, tangible, and legitimate, like the experience we had in Charlotte. If you experience something like that, it makes you realize that not everyone is crazy. There will always be those who put on an act solely for attention or even, dare I say, profit. I've reached a point in my life where I realize that it's not my place to worry about those people. That's between them and God. I'm responsible for and must focus on my own life and how God chooses to move within me.

My heart is truly to see people come out of the darkness into the light, to get past all the religion and theatrics and sincerely find a place where they can lay their burdens at the feet of Christ. I believe it's our faith that activates the power of God in our life. When we have faith or even just the hope of faith, we don't need anything else to approach the throne. We can simply make our requests known.

Roger Breland used to say something during our concerts with TRUTH, and I used to think it was crazy. But now that I'm older and have seen God's hand move, it makes more sense. He said, "Prayer can cause God to do things that He wouldn't ordinarily do." There's something powerful in a corporate call to worship, a corporate gathering of people who are saying, "We're all here together because we need healing, and we believe God can heal us. We are crying out and storming the gates of heaven, asking God to heal us."

I believe God sees that and honors it, and when we take that step of faith, the power of God can move in ways we can't possibly imagine.

FIFTEEN:
THE RENEWAL

During my time with BHM, the demons of my depression started to fight their way to the surface. I had packed down so many failures and so much grief that I couldn't hold it all in any longer.

I was traveling the world, working for this giant ministry, and still trying to figure out what my purpose was. I would have amazing moments of worship where I was on my face before the Lord, but as soon as I got up, those moments subsided and the anxiety came rushing back. The depression was overtaking every aspect of my life.

I was gradually becoming less tolerant of people and even less tolerant of situations at home. I longed to be on an airplane, sitting in a window seat with the blind shut because it was the only time I didn't have to engage with anyone. I was literally losing the ability to hold a relationship together.

During this phase, I started traveling even more, both with BHM and for work with Friends Church once a month in California. I took on the responsibilities of producing my own radio show in Los Angeles and did occasional studio work while I was in town. I was trying to busy myself with whatever I could to distract me from what was really going on inside.

Even on the outside, I was withering away. I had stopped eating and taking care of myself. During the day, I did everything I could to avoid feeling the ache. But at night, when I lay in bed and it was quiet, I could almost feel the darkness creeping in.

When I was home, I went through the motions of the household routine, but I had nothing to give and didn't have the strength to try. One morning after taking Sarah-Clayton to school, I was sitting against the wall on an antique wooden butcher stool in our living room. Stephanie looked at me and said, "Listen, I don't know what to do to help you, but it's obvious that you're dealing with depression. I don't understand. You have a healthy family, a healthy wife, and I don't know what's going on with you. But if you don't go get help, we're going to fall apart."

I didn't know what to say. I was trapped inside myself, wanting to tell her that this man before her wasn't me. I didn't want to act this way, but I had no control over it. Depression had paralyzed me. I couldn't remember a time I had been happy, nor could I see a future where I would ever be happy. I looked at Stephanie with a dull expression on my face and said, "I just don't know anymore."

"You don't know about what?" she asked.

"Anything."

* * *

A huge piece of my depression centered on unprocessed grief over my dad's death. When he passed away in September 2000, my world shifted on its axis. He played a huge role in my life, and his death left an unfillable void. The truth was that I wasn't prepared emotionally for that kind of loss. It began as a slow, downward spiral that would, over time, grow deeper and darker than I ever imagined.

I've learned over the last few years through many hours of counseling that I was probably guilty of putting my dad on an unrealistic pedestal—maybe even placing him where only God should be. It wasn't that I thought my father was perfect. He wasn't. He had a temper, and he made his share of mistakes like everyone else, but he was never afraid to talk about those mistakes. I think that's what made him connect so well with the youth. He didn't make people feel like they had to be perfect before they could come to Jesus. He helped them understand that they could come just as they were and that Jesus could make them into what He wanted them to be.

Coming to terms with his death was a necessary part of getting a handle on my depression. Now that I've come through the other side, I've spent a lot of time researching and trying to better understand what happened to me. Harvard Health Publishing wrote the following about depression, "Chemicals are definitely involved in this process, but it's not a simple matter of one chemical being too low and another being too high. Rather, many chemicals are involved, working both inside and outside the nerve cells. There are millions, even billions, of chemical reactions."[1] Those chemical reactions had been going off inside

---

1. "What Causes Depression," Harvard Health Publishing, June 24, 2019, https://www.health.harvard.edu/mind-and-mood/what-causes-depression.

of me for quite a while and had reached beyond my capacity to manage them alone.

I had a few weeks off from traveling with BHM and felt like taking my family to the beach would help me clear my head—and heart. It was on that beach trip where I hit rock bottom and nearly took my own life. But thankfully, God had another plan.

That moment was the turning point for me. It shook something awake inside of me that had grown complacent in my condition. I finally started looking for ways to heal. I started seeing a counselor who helped me understand what I was going through. He also prescribed antidepressants for me in hopes that they would help balance the chemicals in my mind and stabilize me emotionally.

I had a lot of reservations about taking medicine for my depression because I'd watched people suffer from adverse reactions to them. I also preferred to not take medication in general if I didn't have to. There was also the added concern about taking something in addition to my heart medication. My doctor took the time to find an antidepressant that wouldn't have any adverse reactions yet still be effective. While it took some time to find a balance, I did start to see small improvements.

* * *

Three weeks after I returned home from the beach trip, I got a call that we were doing a two-week tour of Africa with BHM. We would be making various stops in places such as Johannesburg, Cape Town, Durbin, and Côte d'Ivoire, and ending the trip in Equatorial Guinea, which was like so many other places in Africa with extreme poverty and a crumbling infrastructure.

Almost always, the staff traveled separately from PBH, his assistant Marie, and his personal security. Because of that, we were often left to work out any travel issues on our own, and trust me, there were many, and they happened often. This trip was no exception.

We had customs issues in a couple of countries, airline mechanical issues where we were forced to stay overnight in horribly inhospitable situations, and no one in charge traveling with us to help work out any of it. Add the fact that I didn't want to be there in the first place . . . good times.

When we finally flew into the city of Malabo, we were all completely exhausted. It had been the longest couple of weeks we had ever had. The buses picked us up at the airport and drove us through town and along the coast. It looked the same as every other city we had visited in Africa—filthy and run-down. Even the coastline was covered with trash. I eventually avoided looking out the window.

As we continued to drive along the coast, we came to a guard checkpoint that stretched the entire length of the road and all the way to the water on one side and the mountains on the other. There were guards with machine guns posted at every entrance. It was obvious that whatever was on the other side, they didn't want just anyone to have access to it.

As they cleared us to pass through the checkpoint, it was like we were entering another world. On the other side of the checkpoint were massive mansions overlooking the ocean. Beautiful homes with lush green lawns and pristine landscaping dotted the hills and the beach on both sides of the road.

We slowed down and entered gates that led to the Sofitel Hotel where we would be staying. The resort was similar to the one I stayed at on my first trip to Uganda almost four years ago; it was like an oasis. Massive architecture spread the length of a strip of beach with several luxurious pools and a pedestrian bridge that crossed over to a tropical island that had been made into a nature preserve.

The crusade wasn't scheduled until the following day, so we had the early evening and night off to relax and recuperate. I decided to go for a walk along the beach to watch the sunset and explore the island. There were beautiful, whole conch shells scattered along the beach. I'd never seen them so whole and pristine. I decided to sneak a few home for Sarah-Clayton and Stephanie. As I stooped, examining each one, I came across one that was partially buried in the sand and pulled it up. It was completely intact, but the sides were irregularly shaped. The coloring was strange, and there were small points poking out in different directions. It looked like it was trying to be a conch shell but had taken a left-hand turn at some point and never quite got it right.

I looked at that shell and thought, *Buddy, you look like how I feel inside and out. I don't look, act, or sound like everyone else. I have parts of me that stick out, rough edges that never seem to smooth over. Pieces are chipped off here and there.* My life was a mess; *I* was a mess, flawed and imperfect in every way, just like the shell. I slipped it into my pocket.

I had trouble sleeping that night. I couldn't turn my mind off. I wanted to be at home so badly that there was a pit in my stomach. I dozed off and on for a couple of hours. In the morning, I received a text that PBH wanted the entire staff to meet for lunch in the hotel restaurant.

I got to the restaurant and took a seat at the farthest spot I could find from PBH, who always sat at the head of the table. I wasn't in the mood for small talk or stories. There were always so many stories. As the rest of the staff started to arrive, no one noticed my strategic choice of seat or they would have pointed it out. They all just sat around me and started to order.

While we were waiting for our food, people were commenting on how beautiful the beach was and how crazy it was to drive through the checkpoint and enter an entirely different world. The food started to arrive, and the banter died down quite a bit as everyone began to eat.

During a moment of extended silence, from the other end of the table, I heard PBH's booming voice say, "JOOODDDYYY!"

I was sitting next to one of the large security guys, and I slid behind his giant shoulder, hoping it would somehow hide me. Obviously, PBH knew I was there, so my hiding was pointless. He kindly but firmly announced again across the long table, "JOOODY, I see you, brother!" As he continued to cut the food on his plate without looking up, he said, "Jody, today I want you to pray for the sick."

That was all he said, and then he went back to eating and talking with the staff near him. I peered at the people around me, and while they all continued to eat, a few glanced at me with expressions like they were trying to contain both laughter and fear.

I had no idea how to pray for the sick, at least not the way he and the healers on staff did it. I was sitting next to Jim who had been the pastor's right-hand man for many years. He turned to me and said, "Don't worry about it. I'll walk you through it. Just be downstairs and ready to go to the venue at 3:30."

I was somewhat familiar with the prayer procedure, having watched it dozens of times in various places all over the world. The prayer team went to the venue several hours before the event started, and people would be in the audience requesting prayer for specific miracles. A team member would pray one-on-one with them and afterward ask them to come onstage that night to testify about how God had healed them.

I have to be forthright and say that in the nearly four years I had been with BHM, I hadn't seen anything that could be considered a miracle take place before my eyes.

At 3:30, we left the hotel and made the drive through the checkpoint and back to the other side of town where the event was being held. We pulled up to a large soccer arena and drove through the gates to a private, rear area that led to a group of holding rooms and PBH's green room, or the Dove Room, as the staff called it.

At this specific venue, the Dove Room was the only air-conditioned room in the entire stadium, and it was over 100 degrees outside. No one but PBH and his personal staff and security was allowed to go into the Dove Room unless PBH asked them to come in. So we went into the normal staff green room and prepared ourselves to go into the crowd and pray.

Something that may not be widely known about me is that I have a touch of OCD, especially when it comes to cleanliness. (For the record, I don't think it's nearly as bad as my wife makes it out to be.) I've been known to shower three times in one day, particularly during the summer months. Even before the worldwide COVID-19 pandemic, I carried antibacterial gel and wipes with me at all times. When traveling, especially internationally, I wiped down every surface before I sat down or touched anything. That is just how I am.

So since it was a thousand degrees outside and Africa was not the cleanest place on earth, I was not looking forward to going into the huddled masses. And to add insult to injury, we had to wear suits and ties. I mean, why not just asphyxiate me now and get it over with?

As we moved out of the green room and to the stands, I could feel the wall of heat and the smell of, well, Africa, hit me in the face. Needless to say, my attitude was not what it should have been for someone headed into prayer time. As we rounded the corner, I was blown away by what I saw. The stands were packed with more than 10,000 people crammed into this soccer arena. I became overwhelmed.

Jim had failed to give me explicit instructions on how to do this. I mean, I knew how to pray, but I had never, ever prayed for someone to be healed and then expected it to happen instantaneously. I still wasn't sure I even believed that was possible because, as I said, I had never seen it. Growing up in a Baptist church, we did pray for people who were sick. We anointed them with oil, and the deacons laid hands on them. I saw it happen a lot, but there always seemed to be an underlying attitude of *We're going to go ahead and pray for you because it's what we do, but it probably won't make any real difference.* Maybe that was just my perspective as a young person. Like the old expression goes, *You pray for the sick while you prepare for them to die.*

From the stage, the local pastor announced in French, the national language, that Benny Hinn's staff was here and ready to pray with them for healing. He asked people to raise their hands if they needed healing, and someone from the staff would come and pray with them. When he said that, I'm pretty sure 9,500 hands shot up. There were only 12 of us to pray with them, and I chuckled under my breath, thinking, *Well, that's not gonna happen.*

As we started moving toward the crowd, one of the BHM staff members said to me, "When you go up to pray for someone, ask them what they need God to do, and then pray with them for it. If God doesn't heal them right away, just tell them, 'Keep praying, your miracle is on the way,' and move on." I started calling that the "company line." They assigned an interpreter to me because I don't speak French, and then they sent me on my way.

I turned to the crowd and saw thousands of hands waving for my attention. I had no idea where to start. People were waving for me to come to them, looking at me like they couldn't breathe and

I was giving away oxygen. I start walking down the aisle through the audience with my interpreter and Brian, my security person.

As I walked through the crowd trying to decide where to start, my first thought wasn't about praying for their diseases. I'm ashamed to say it, but my mind was focused instead on how filthy everyone was, the unbearable heat, and the horrible smell wafting in the air. I also was wondering about communicable diseases. That's where my mind was. I was more concerned about myself and my well-being than what I was there to do.

I walked up to a woman who was probably in her late 50s or early 60s. She had a glassed-over look on her face. I asked her through the interpreter, "What do you need God to do for you?" She responded in French, "I have pain." I asked her to be more specific, to tell me where the pain was, and she replied, "Everywhere."

I looked more closely at her and noticed her body was tremoring slightly as if she were chilled. When I put my hand on her shoulder, she flinched as though she were scared of me. I asked her if I could pray for her, and she said yes. I don't remember the specific words I prayed, but it was something like *Lord, she's in pain, please take her pain away, in the name of Jesus, and heal her if it be Your will.*

Afterward, I asked her how she felt, and she said, "The pain is gone." Wow! This was easier than I thought. I leaned toward her and asked, "Would you be willing to testify during the service to what God has done?" She said yes, and they escorted her over to the side of the stage to sit where she could be called up during the service. She was still shuddering, and to me, nothing visible had changed. There was something strange about her, but I couldn't put my finger on it.

I made my way to five or six more people and repeated the same things I had done with the first woman. Nothing happened.

It was so hot. Around me, people were hollering and flailing, and some were pulling at me. I could feel my composure slipping and my frustration growing. I noticed the interpreter and Brian were getting frustrated as well. I looked at Brain and said, "I'm done, man. I don't wanna do this anymore. Let's go back."

We turned around and started to make a beeline for the backstage area. As we walked through the crowd, I did my best not to make eye contact with anyone so I wouldn't have to stop again. Brian even moved a couple of people out of the way to clear a path. As I was nearing the front of the crowd, I happened to look up and saw a young woman waving to get my attention. She had on a long, red-and-green dress. She was filthy but beautiful and tall. She couldn't have been older than 25.

As I was walking closer to her, she moved to her left slightly, and I saw a short, elderly woman standing behind her, holding on to her dress. Even from that distance, I could tell something was wrong with her. She had her face turned downward, and when she looked up, I saw it. Her eyes were covered in white. This old woman was blind.

The minute I saw the old woman's eyes, I knew someone was about to ask me to pray for the woman's sight to return. I thought, *You've got to be kidding me. I don't know how to do that!* And instantly I heard a voice say, "This is not about you." I turned and looked at Brian. "Did you say something?" He shook his head and looked at me like I was crazy. I figured I'd just overheard someone around us.

When I reached the girl, she introduced herself to me and then, through the interpreter, said, "This is my grandmother. She has not seen since she was 12 years old, and I would like God to restore her sight."

In that moment, every single insecurity came rushing in, and I could feel the ache in my stomach start to move to my throat.

Three weeks earlier, I had been standing in the ocean chest-deep, contemplating ending my own existence. I was in no condition to heal some woman's blindness. *I don't know how to do that.* This time the voice was much louder and spoke with more authority. *Jody, this is not about you.* The hairs on the back of my neck rose. I had never heard the audible voice of God before, but I had no doubt who was speaking these words to me. I believe that was the moment when something inside of me started to change.

I remembered that in the Bible when Jesus healed the blind man, He spit on the sand and made mud, and then applied the mud to the man's eyes with His hands. I didn't think about making mud with spit at that point, but I did feel it was important to touch the old woman's eyes while I prayed. So I asked the girl, "Will you please ask your grandmother if I can put my hands on her eyes?" I don't know why I didn't have the interpreter ask the grandmother directly, but I was so nervous that I was shaking, so I don't think I was thinking clearly.

The interpreter asked the girl, and she asked her grandmother. The grandmother agreed, so I reached down. The woman wasn't much taller than five feet, and I placed my hands on her eyes.

While I prayed, I felt like at any moment I was going to come apart at the seams. Overwhelmed by fear of making a mistake or saying something wrong, I said, "Lord, I know that You can heal this woman." Then I said something about how He'd healed the blind man and how that same power is available to us today. I believed every word of the prayer coming out of my mouth. Then as I was getting ready to finish, I said, "You have made it crystal clear to me today that this is not about me. I realize I can't do any of this under my own strength, so I'm just asking for You to be God and heal this woman if it be Your will. In Jesus's name, amen."

182

I took my hands off her eyes. My heart was thumping hard with deep beats. I don't know what I expected would happen next, maybe angels appearing and singing the "Hallelujah Chorus" or maybe a rainbow arching across the sky and doves flying overhead. I can't lie and say that I didn't have huge expectations based on the fact that I knew I had heard the voice of God.

But instead . . . there was nothing.

I thought, *Well, womp-womp. That was anticlimactic*, and I felt an instant disappointment. I turned to the granddaughter, and through the interpreter, I was about to deliver the company line, but before I could get the words out of my mouth, the old woman began to scream—a bloodcurdling scream like she was in pain. I thought, *Oh dear Jesus, I have killed this woman.* She was cupping her eyes with her hands, patting on them, and wailing.

I started freaking out. Everybody around us was freaking out. Brian went into a defensive position because he thought she was about to go crazy. You have to understand, there were 10,000 people in this arena, and they were African, so they're naturally exuberant anyway, but the volume of this woman's scream was so unique and pervasive that people stopped what they were doing and turned to watch what was happening.

The granddaughter reached over, grabbed her grandma's hands, and pulled them away from her eyes. I watched as the woman opened her eyes, tears streaming down her cheeks while her white eyes looked up at the blue sky. Then I saw something I will never forget, something I have thought about every day since it happened. I watched as the white film that covered this old woman's eyes began dissolving into her pupils. She began blinking, and her eyes started watering again. She turned slowly and blinked several times, over and over, and then grabbed her granddaughter's face and said, *"Je te vois. Je te vois!"*

The interpreter looked at me and mouthed the translation, "I see you. I see you." I didn't need a translation to know what I'd just seen. I watched this woman get healed right in front of me. Within seconds, all the people gathered around us and went completely crazy. They all started shouting, and before we could respond, chaos erupted. People started pushing, shoving, and surrounding the woman and her granddaughter. Brian pulled me out of the way as people started to push in. I looked at him and said, "Get me out of here, now."

I felt bad for leaving so quickly. I didn't get to thank the interpreter. We walked back to the green room, and Brian took me into the Dove Room. PBH's assistant was in the room and immediately started to fuss about coming into Pastor's room. She stopped when she saw both of our faces, and I gave her that don't-even-start look. She just turned around and left the room.

Brian and I sat down on opposite sides of the room and stared at each other. I'd never been here before—in a place where something had happened that I couldn't put words to. Even in my deepest despair, I could always find words to express my heartbreak or words to cry out to God. This time, I was speechless.

Brian saw everything, and he was as stunned as I was, if not more. He was former Special Forces in the military and had been through a lot, some that I knew about and much more that he never shared. More than an hour passed before either of us spoke. Brian said, "I have taken life with my own hands, but I've never seen anybody give life before."

"I didn't do that." I was adamant. No way was I taking credit for something I knew I didn't do. I hadn't felt anything different when I prayed for her. There had been no tingling. Time hadn't stood still. I hadn't felt any healing power leave my body. In fact, I'd felt nothing.

The service that night went on as planned. It was a long one, but they were all long. Toward the end of the service, the healing line came up to share. That night was a crazy one, to say the least. Witches came onstage posing as having been healed and trying to curse PBH. The first woman I had prayed with, the one who had pain everywhere, ended up being possessed—something else I had never seen before until that night.

I think everyone on the platform spent most of the night in shock, and much of the evening ended up being a blur. However, I do remember vividly the once-blind grandmother coming up onstage with her granddaughter. I was standing back, singing in the corner of the stage, and I watched as through an interpreter they told her story. I sat down on my chair in the corner and began to sob. I looked over at Brian, and while he was trying to maintain his focus, I'm pretty sure I saw a tear fall down the side of his cheek. I never told anyone on the team that I had been the one to pray over her. I'm not sure they would have believed me. It didn't make a difference to me whether they knew or not because, just like God said, it wasn't about me.

God reveals Himself to each person differently, often during their hour of greatest need. Moses heard God through a burning bush. Belshazzar saw writing on the wall by God's own hand. I would say these are extreme ways that God revealed Himself. That's not usually the case for most of us. I spent my entire life limiting how God spoke to me. But God is limitless. His love for us goes beyond any restrictions we try to impose on Him.

Maybe we don't hear Him talking to us because we don't want to hear what He has to say. You know the old expression *The truth hurts*. Well, God is all truth. I was in such a dark place in my life, and I had started to feel like maybe God wasn't all I had believed He was. By God speaking to me and allowing me to be part of that miracle, it was like He was saying to me, *I'm real, I'm here, and I am powerful and working. You need to trust Me with your life; your trust is well-placed.*

The next day, we flew home. I couldn't sleep as I usually do on flights. I kept replaying the experience over and over in my mind—seeing the grandmother's eyes, remembering the shouts of praise from the people around her, feeling for the first time in my life the certainty of God's love for me. He loved me enough to let me be part of something *that* special, *that* supernatural.

I'm thrilled she was healed. I'm thrilled she got to see her granddaughter for the first time. That memory will live with me forever. But more than anything, I know I serve a God who is able to do immeasurably more than I could ever ask or imagine. He's a healing God; He's a powerful God; and if nothing else, it cemented my calling forever because I knew as I flew home from Africa that I would spend the rest of my life telling people about what God had done, what God is able to do.

Some of you reading these words may be saying to yourself, *I don't believe that.* I get it. I was just like you until that point of my life. I spent almost four years leading worship for a healing ministry I really didn't believe in. But if there is one thing I have learned about God in the last several years, it's that He does not need my permission to be who He is. Luke 18:27 (NIV) says, "What is impossible with man is possible with God." I needed to believe in a God who was more than just the religion I was raised to believe. So God, on one extremely hot afternoon in Africa, proved Himself to me. He didn't have to, but because He loves me, He did.

Do I think He heals all the time? No, I don't think He does. Do I know why He doesn't heal all the time? No, I don't. But I'm okay not having all those answers. I've been given a supernatural glimpse of His power. I know it exists, and I also know His heart. He is a compassionate God, so if He chooses not to use that power, He must have His reasons.

When my father was in his hospital bed, unconscious, my wife prayed, believing he would be completely healed. She was so convinced that she told me several times, "I know he's going to be okay!" Obviously, that did not happen, and I spent years struggling with why God would tell her He was going to let him live only to take him. She struggled, too, because she believed it with her entire being. I still don't have an answer for that. But what I do know now is that God is real and does have a reason. Part of being a person of faith is placing our trust in His plan and trusting the process, even if it's painful at times. His plan continues to unfold, and providence marches on.

I'll say one more thing about healing. Not all Christians are comfortable hearing about a miracle. When I go to other churches to sing or as part of an event, I ask if I can share my story, and many have declined. You've read enough of this book to not be surprised when I tell you I share it anyway because I'm responsible to do so.

I knew that God was starting to open new doors of ministry for me and that my time with BHM was coming to a close. I only took a couple more trips with them after the Africa tour. One of my last trips with him was to the Holy Land. I wasn't asked to go to the Holy Land, but I offered my services because I felt a strong pull to be there. After what happened in Africa, I needed to walk where Christ walked and be where He performed His miracles.

I spent the first three and a half years of my time with Benny Hinn asking why I was there. Like so many other times in my life, I was out of place. I didn't fit, and I always felt awkward. Then Africa happened at the precise moment I needed it most. And I knew that was exactly why God had me there. He needed to prove Himself to me in a way I would have never experienced had I been sitting behind a desk in the United States.

I decided to leave BHM when I saw some questionable things happening that I disagreed with, specifically all the prosperity preaching and the high-pressure offering tactics. There was a guy I won't name who came in and give the offering sermon at every event. He pushed everyone to "sow a $1,000 seed," and if they did, they would see whatever miracle they were hoping for in seven days. Every time he gave that sermon, I cringed and squirmed in my chair. I knew much of what he said was not biblical, and I watched people come forward and give the last $1,000 they had so they could "unlock their miracle." It took about three events for me to realize it was time to go.

Sadly, PBH didn't have much to say when I left. Relationally speaking, he kept almost everyone on his staff at arm's length if not farther. As I said before, he was shielded from everything and nearly everyone. His staff inflated attendance numbers and offering totals to keep him from losing his cool. He was always surrounded by an abundance of security, which seemed excessive in my opinion. All that contributed to him being inaccessible. I don't think anyone ever really knew where they stood with him.

But that doesn't matter to me anymore. I never needed or wanted the approval of Benny Hinn. But there is no question why God allowed me to be part of his ministry. That one, single moment turned my life around forever and lit a fire within me that will never be extinguished, and for that I will be forever grateful.

SIXTEEN:
THE NEW BEGINNING

God's timing is always perfect. The week I decided to leave BHM, I was contacted by a man named Landon Beene. He was part owner of StowTown Records and IMC Concerts, both enterprises rooted primarily in the Southern gospel genre.

Landon was very complimentary and familiar with my time with TRUTH and Avalon. He told me about his vision to start a mixed trio that would have a more contemporary Southern gospel sound. He already had two of the three singers in place and needed another tenor. He wanted to know if I would be interested.

The other two members were Doug Anderson and his then fiancée, TaRanda Greene. Both had solid Southern gospel roots and had been successful in other groups. They also both had well-established solo careers. While I was fairly familiar with the Southern gospel genre, I never pictured myself being part of it.

In fact, when Landon and I spoke initially, he asked me if I ever thought about being part of another group again, and I'm pretty sure I told him nope.

I talked to Stephanie about it, and her first response was, "Oh no!" The thought of being with a new group and walking down that artist road again was scary. Mentally and emotionally, I had turned a major corner, and I felt ready for full-time ministry again, but would a new group be a good idea? I mean, I didn't even know these people.

Landon suggested that we meet and get to know each other. He said that he and TaRanda would be coming through Nashville in a week or so and would like to meet for dinner.

A week later, I pulled up to J. Alexander's and sat in the parking lot trying to calm my nerves. It wasn't an audition, but it felt like it was. I had heard things about Landon and TaRanda—things that made me question whether or not I should be there. It was nothing earth-shattering, but it was gossip that brought their character into question. But who was I to lecture anyone on character flaws?

Within 15 minutes of meeting them both, I knew what I had heard was wrong. They were honest, real, and had a story. They spoke to me about brokenness and healing and what they wanted to see God do with this new group. We laughed and told stories, and I left that meeting feeling like I had known them for years. I went back to my car, called Stephanie, and said, "Welp, looks like I'm going to be in another group."

Over the next couple of days, I thought and prayed about what I was considering. I hadn't met Doug yet and had not heard either one of them sing. We also had never sung together as a trio, so I had no idea if our voices would blend well. I called a friend of mine, a worship pastor in Alabama, and told him, "I just met with Landon and TaRanda, and I'm considering being part of a new trio with them (we didn't have a name at the time), but I've never heard her sing."

Before I finished the sentence, my friend said, "You've never heard her sing? Bro, she's a beast! I'm going to send you a link right now of a song. You are going to die." I clicked on a YouTube link for TaRanda Greene, "I Walked Today Where Jesus Walked," and sat in my car and sobbed. It was a live performance with no tuning and no editing. It was almost flawless and one of the most powerful vocals I had ever heard. She is truly one of the finest singers in the industry. Fast-forward to when I was singing with her, and I have to admit that I had some insecurity because I don't have the kind of consistency and control that she has. I don't know anyone who does. Like her or not, Celine Dion was for a very long time the finest vocalist in the industry, but TaRanda is better.

A couple of nights later, we all met at Wayne Haun's home just outside Nashville where I met Doug Anderson. He was very kind and had the type of attitude and personality that puts a person immediately at ease. Wayne made dinner for us, and we sat around a large table and ate and talked about our lives and careers. Wayne is an accomplished writer and producer and also part of the StowTown Records family.

After dinner, Wayne suggested that we gather around his piano. We already knew we liked each other, so it was probably best to see if we could sing together. We went to his music room and gathered around his baby grand. Wayne sat down at the keys, and they all looked at me. I was like, "What?" They chuckled and asked if I knew any of "their" music because they were all from the Southern gospel genre, and of course, I was not. I assured them that I knew plenty, that I had grown up in a Southern Baptist church that had gospel sings all the time. I had also sung in a Southern gospel quartet in college, so I wasn't completely unfamiliar with the genre.

I started throwing songs out there that I knew or had sung, and they were like, "Oh my gosh, I can't believe you know that song!" Of course, they all had a vast knowledge of the genre and started to sing songs I had never heard before. But for the most part, we found quite a bit of common ground musically, and our voices meshed much better than I thought they would, probably in large part because all of us had sung with groups and knew what it meant to blend with other singers.

For some reason, I brought up a Michael English song that was on his first record, a song called "His Heart Is Big Enough." Wayne started to play it, and I just started to sing. Doug added a part, and then TaRanda started singing the third above me, and just like that, the group came to life. It was one of those epiphany moments that you can't orchestrate or plan. I've maybe experienced a moment like that twice in my life. It was like the stars aligned and the heavens opened up, and for an instant, God was shining down on us.

We sang songs like that for hours. We somehow ended up lying under the piano head-to-head, talking about what we wanted this group to be and how each of us had longed for something like this in our lives. We shared what we wanted God to do with the group and how excited we were about all the possibilities. We had something in common. We'd all been broken by choices or situations in our lives. We decided we wanted to be a voice for the broken. We wanted to share God's voice with people who shared our scars. We wanted people to realize they were not alone in their suffering.

As I drove home that night, I felt encouraged and humbled that God had shown up, and I knew we were onto something special.

Being part of this new group meant I had to start traveling again. That was something that would be difficult for my wife and family. Stephanie has always tried hard to be supportive even though I was constantly saying goodbye and missing important family moments. My life as a traveling musician had definitely strained our family life in the past, and though she's never said so, I think if she could have changed one thing about our marriage, it would have been that I had not been gone so much. However, I think Stephanie also knew that as difficult as it was with me away, it was the life I was called to. How in the world could I preach the gospel with the gifts God had given me if I didn't actually leave home?

Thanks to Landon's connections as a promoter, we were able to get our feet wet on a few tours as a new artist while we were in and out of the studio recording our debut release. Everything was coming together really well, but we had one problem: we didn't have a name. Amazingly, we went nearly a year without one. We tossed around several ideas, but all of them were either taken or just didn't seem right. It was getting frustrating because we had finished a record, it was being mixed and mastered, and we had no idea what to put on the cover.

One day while TaRanda was reading her Bible on the bus, she read the story in John 2 where Christ performed His first documented miracle at the wedding at Cana.

If you're not familiar with the story, here's the short and skinny of it. Jesus and Mary attended a wedding, and the host ran out of wine. Mary came to Jesus and said, "Hey, we're out of wine. Do something." And Jesus looked at her and said, "Woman, my time has not yet come."

I'm pretty sure that Mary, being a mother, a Jewish mother at that, gave him a look that said, "I don't care about your time. I said, 'Do something.'" Jesus loved His mom, and I know I'm taking creative license here, but I imagine Jesus and God conferred with one another (they probably talk to each other on a constant basis if we get into the whole idea of the Trinity), and Jesus said, "God, maybe now's as good a time as any for Me to pull out a miracle." And God said, "Sure, why not?"

The Bible TaRanda was using was a study Bible, and it had a section that went into detail about what it would have been like to attend a wedding back then. There was specific mention of the barrels or vessels that people used to wash their hands and feet in before they came into the wedding feast. The commentary said that most likely they were the vessels Jesus used when He turned the water into wine.

TaRanda started thinking that the water He used was most likely dirty because it was used to wash everyone's dusty hands and feet. Typically, when you see pictures of this story, they always portray Jesus walking up to a beautiful golden goblet and touching it, turning water to wine. From what she was reading, that may not have been how it went down. When He said, "Bring Me some earthen vessels," they probably brought the vessels that were already full of dirty water.

TaRanda started thinking that maybe some of the vessels had been chipped or cracked and overall not very pretty. However, in the hands of the Master, He made these earthen vessels into something beautiful and the filth inside into something perfect. The wine was probably the finest ever consumed, and that's what they drank for the rest of the wedding ceremony.

As TaRanda continued reading, she began to fall apart when she realized that God took something that was dirty and broken and repurposed it for something incredible. That's exactly what we wanted our group to do. We had talked about wanting to be the voice for the broken. After all, we were three people who had been filled with dirty water, and Jesus found us, cleaned us, and repurposed us to do His work. We wanted everyone to know that regardless of their past, Jesus could do the same for them. We decided that day that we would call our group Cana's Voice.

I will always be eternally grateful to Landon Beene for giving me a second chance to do music. He came along in a season of my life after the beach incident when I was just coming into my own emotionally and spiritually through counseling. Landon was obedient in that moment to reach out to me and give me another chance at ministry. I surely wouldn't be doing any kind of ministry full-time if he hadn't given me a chance.

While signing a contract with StowTown Records for Cana's Voice, I was also able to negotiate two solo records. I was honored to be part of the group, and I also really wanted to build my own, viable solo ministry like TaRanda and Doug had done. Cana's Voice would only have 30 or 40 dates a year, and I wouldn't be able to support my family on that. I also had personal things on my heart I wanted to say that I couldn't necessarily do in a group. Landon kindly agreed.

My first solo record was called *Keep Breathing*. The title was born out of some advice I received from my counselor after the incident at the beach. In one of our first sessions, I told him, "Listen, I know something is off in me. I can't rationalize through these problems in my life." The counselor asked, "Well, what do you want from me then?" I told him I wasn't sure. "But I'll tell you what I don't want. I don't want you to quote Scripture to me because I cannot handle hearing Jeremiah 29:11 one more time. And honestly, I've heard all the Scriptures that could be quoted in this situation. What I need is tangible, physical help."

He looked at me and said, "Jody, I can help you, and I know God can help you, but nobody can help you if you stop breathing. You have to keep breathing because you have a responsibility to yourself, to your family, and to your God to keep going. I guarantee you, when you get to the other side of this, there is going to be a harvest that's reaped. You're going to be able to help so many people. It doesn't seem possible now, but you have to trust me."

For nearly two years after that, anytime I posted something online, I added the hashtag *#keepbreathing* at the end of the post. Many people wrote, "I love that" or "I needed that," while other people said, "What's this 'keep breathing' crap? Why do you keep saying that?" I can't be sure why I got negative responses to a simple hashtag phrase except maybe people expected me to always be a happy, funny guy. I was going through a dark period, and I just don't think people were ready for that or knew how to respond. I kept it up because that hashtag wasn't for them; it was for the ones who were struggling like I was.

People reached out to me and said, "I've never had anyone tell me to keep breathing." I was amazed because most of these people were born and raised in the church. They'd never been told by a spiritual authority that they have to keep pressing on, keep moving forward. No one had said not to give up on God's plan for their life because He never gives up on them.

But the saddest part for me was the fact that all these veteran churchgoers hadn't been allowed to admit that they struggled with depression. The topic had become taboo inside the church walls, and to admit to dealing with depression would bring judgment, ridicule, and shaming from the people who should have been helping them heal in the first place.

I made sure that every song on that solo record was chosen or written based on experiences I'd had. One of the songs, "In the Presence of Jesus," talks about how anything is possible with God. He is still a miracle worker. He's able to do more than we could ever fathom. That song was born out of the experience of seeing the African woman regain her sight.

The song "Me" was written about my experience that night on the beach, about being in the water and staring up at heaven, feeling worthless and like God had forgotten me. The lyrics describe how when Jesus hung on the cross, He thought of me and every single person by name. He thought of us all and bore every sin we would ever commit. It was the price He was willing to pay because He loves us all that much.

It's hard to put all that into one record, but I feel like we did, and I was very pleased with the final product. The bummer is that I don't think it ended up selling as much as StowTown had hoped, and that hurt because they had invested so much of their time and belief into the project. Months after the record was released, many people had no idea it had even come out. The marketing for the album just wasn't there. It seemed like the only people who knew I had released a record were the people who followed me on social media, which at the time I was just starting to build.

That wasn't StowTown's fault. It was 2016 and nearly impossible to market a Christian record if you didn't already have a solid social media following. The traditional ways of marketing a record had changed drastically because we didn't have brick-and-mortar Christian music stores anymore. Christian publications were no longer in print to advertise in. Success is placed squarely on the shoulders of both the artist and the label's social media platforms. It's not ideal, but it's the way things have evolved.

In my earlier days in CCM, Christian radio played a huge role in the discoverability of new music to the masses, probably too big of a role. It singlehandedly broke out Avalon as an artist in the late '90s and then singlehandedly destroyed us as an artist in the early 2000s. That's not me calling them out from my seat on the bitter bus, those are just the facts. Sadly, it's still that way today, although CCM stations aren't as prevalent. When I was coming up in the industry, there were giant Christian radio stations all over the country. Now there's K-LOVE, which is a large syndicated station, and some smaller stations in cities.

The culture has changed toward Christian music, and the rotation on Christian radio has grown smaller and smaller, filled with only a handful of artists who are played over and over. Let me reiterate, I am not bitter because I have *surely* had my share of radio success, and Southern gospel radio has been very kind to Cana's Voice. However, many people have told me how frustrating it is because they never hear new music on the radio, and because of that, people don't tune in as much as they used to.

StowTown Records is predominantly a Southern gospel label, so people viewed *Keep Breathing* as a Southern gospel release. Consequently, I didn't get any mainstream CCM radio airtime. I refuse to worry about that kind of stuff anymore because that's not why I'm here now. *Keep Breathing* was about having something substantial I could give to people, something to help me tell my story.

It continues to sell online, and I'm thankful I have it. It's funny because it released in 2016, and I still have people who see it online and tell me they had no idea I made a record. Thankfully, people are still being introduced to it and still buying it.

That same year, Cana's Voice came out with our album *This Changes Everything*. Later that year, I went into the studio to record an EP (extended play) of Christmas songs. The album, called *Christmastime*, was literally a dream come true for me. I'd wanted to do something like that since I was a boy, and the great thing about Christmas music is that it's timeless. Avalon's Christmas record *Joy* is still a top-selling record every year on digital platforms, and it came out in 2000.

I wanted my Christmas record to be something people could put on while they're decorating the tree. I wanted it to be chill and a little jazzy. Most of the vocals I actually recorded in the studio at the same time the band was laying down their parts. That's something you don't get to do very often because the tracks are usually done first. Some of it was just scratch vocals, and I ended up going back to fix a little here and there later.

I sang through the songs while the trio played them. That trio was comprised of three of the most amazing players in Nashville— Danny O'Lanerty on upright bass, Scott Williamson on drums, and Jason Webb on keys with David Cleveland making an appearance on one song as well. It was truly the dream team, and they were the only players we used on most of the record. The album had a couple of full production songs as well, which meant Wayne Haun, who produced the project, had a full orchestra play on them. However, my favorite songs are the ones that are simply just the trio or David.

Cana's Voice was moving along at a fair clip and staying as busy as we could, given everyone's busy solo schedules. We had been touring our first record for a couple of years, and the time had come for us to follow up the strong response from our first release with a second one. We decided to meet in Nashville with one of our pro-ducers-arrangers and come up with a plan for the second record.

In the middle of that meeting, I got a phone call from Greg Long. Since he seldom called me, I figured it was probably impor-tant and excused myself to answer the call. We'd spoken a couple of times before, but not a lot, so I was definitely curious.

After some small talk and friendly banter, Greg said, "Well, we've been talking a lot about what the next chapter of Avalon looks like." He'd been talking to Jay DeMarcus from the country group Rascal Flatts. He was the owner of a new Christian label called Red Street Records. He and Don Koch, who was also part of Red Street and slated to produce Avalon's next record, apparently all agreed that they wanted my sound back in the group. He asked me if I would ever consider coming back to Avalon. I told him I was honored that people wanted me back but would have to talk to Stephanie about it. I was a very different person than I was 11 years ago. In my mind I was thinking, *No way!*

He said he understood and wanted to know when he should follow up. Something you should know about Greg is that he's a stickler about certain things. For instance, if you tell him you'll let him know something by Tuesday, he's texting you Tuesday morning wanting an answer. I told him, "Give me a week." He agreed, and we left it at that.

I came home that night, and Stephanie and I sat on the couch and watched *The Bachelor* because my wife is obsessed with it. I, on the other hand, don't get it. I mean, marriage after like two dates? Whatever. I usually try to sneak upstairs and watch something sci-fi, but on that night, she was screaming and laughing about whatever it was that was unfolding during "the most dramatic rose ceremony ever." Once the commercial came on, I turned to her on the couch and said, "I want to talk to you about something," and she replied, "Uh-oh."

"I spoke to Greg Long today. They want to know if I'd consider coming back to Avalon. What do you think?" I was sort of wincing like she might hit me or something. She stared quietly at me for a second and then said, "I think that's unbelievable! You're crazy if you don't do that. That's the music you were created to make." She paused. "But it needs to be done differently than last time. You can't be gone 280 days a year. You have a daughter, and we have responsibilities. But if we can work through the scheduling, I think it's something you need to do."

One week later, on the dot, Greg called. I told him I'd like to move forward with this idea and see how it goes. That began a long and interesting journey to try to breathe new life back into a group that had been out of the spotlight for 12 years. I made an agreement with Cana's Voice that they would be my first priority, and then I set out to be part of two music groups.

Avalon's first single came out in October 2019 with the intention of releasing a record shortly after. Because we didn't get the reception at Christian radio we had hoped on the first single, the label decided to push the release date back to February 2020.

Little did we know that 2020 would be an awful year to try to relaunch an artist or release a record. The album released on Valentine's Day, and we began touring a month later. However, because of the worldwide COVID-19 pandemic, all tour dates were canceled, and we were forced to come off the road. We didn't have the support of Christian radio. We didn't have the support of a tour to promote. An unforeseen global pandemic was sweeping the world. Needless to say, it was horrible timing.

Balancing both groups was precarious at times as well. It was difficult because I wanted to be fair to Cana's Voice, but the responsibilities of relaunching Avalon were making it difficult, and there were communication breakdowns that were mostly my fault. I owed Landon and Cana's Voice so much. I wouldn't be back doing music at all if it hadn't been for them. However, they would have never wanted me in the group if I hadn't been in Avalon first.

I have no knowledge of anyone who has ever attempted to be in two touring music groups at the same time. I'm sure it's been done, but I'm also certain that the reason I haven't heard about it is because the person who tried to do it went down in flames.

I've learned a lot through this process, mostly that communication is key and that both groups need to be aware of what the other is doing at all times. I struggled with that in the beginning, and it made things difficult. Cana's Voice suffered the most.

SEVENTEEN:
THE PURPOSE

I came across a quote a few years ago that goes something like this: "Some people when they hear your story contract. Others upon hearing your story expand; and this is how you know."

When we see someone with a limp or obvious scarring, we either turn away because they make us uncomfortable or we are drawn to them because we know they have a story to tell. I used to be more like the person who turned away. I didn't want my feelings to be inconvenienced, and I certainly didn't want to feel uncomfortable. However, the older I get, the more I'm drawn to people with scars. Their stories give me hope. Their perseverance inspires me to keep going.

I wrote this book with the hope that people will read my story and press in. By showing you my scars and sharing my struggles, maybe you will be inspired to ask the hard questions you've always needed answers to. The questions I needed to ask and have answered centered on the idea of perfection. I spent the first 45 years of my life believing I had to be perfect and I had to be holy. If I didn't accomplish that goal, I was a failure. I was so focused on this mindset that it resulted in an unbearable amount of pressure, a pressure so strong that it nearly broke me permanently.

The last few years, I have shared as openly as I could about my struggles with depression and anxiety. I've also been as honest as I could about my insecurities and flaws. In doing so, I've learned that there is a limit to how much honesty people can handle, especially Christians.

While so many want to believe that grace is extended to them in abundance, we aren't always so great about extending that same grace to people whose sins and struggles look different from ours. There is an unspoken line that separates us and has made churches more like theaters than hospitals.

Being part of a fellowship of believers comes with an unrealistic expectation of needing to portray this perception of perfection to be accepted and welcomed. While many churches say, "If you're broken, hurt, depressed, or flawed, you're welcome here," there is still an underlying pressure to get your act together quickly if you want to start serving and become a regular member.

Yet the people who hold leadership positions are battling their own dysfunctions and their own demons every day. This lack of tolerance for the less than perfect is why they hide their sins to the detriment of everything. They are terrified to admit it because others will consider them ill-equipped to lead.

I have had close friends get so overwhelmed with the charade that they could no longer take the pressure. And because they couldn't see any other way out, they took their own lives, all because they weren't permitted to be what we all are—human.

I know that right now someone is reading this, and they are in the proverbial water, chest-deep. If that person is you, I want you to know I've been where you are. I've felt that pull to walk deeper until the water drowns out the pain. But when I say I'm so thankful I didn't, that's not just Christianese; it's the truth. I'm so grateful that God turned me around and brought me back to the shore because I was literally months from the breakthrough I was so desperately looking for.

My mental health isn't perfect. I still have moments of anxiety and depression. But I have come through to the other side, and when I'm at my weakest, I'm reminded that there is a strength available to me that is not my own and is limitless. I have survived my fair share of dark days. I'm not about to let all that fighting and struggle be in vain. There is a reason for it all. Whether it's to keep me focused, draw me closer to God, or just to make me more compassionate to others, I know that nothing is wasted. I also know that I have what it takes to survive what's ahead and finally feel like I'm brave enough to share the lessons I've learned. You're holding the fruit of all that in your hands.

People may pick up this book and start reading in the hopes that I will air all my dirty laundry for the world to see. Maybe they're looking for confirmation of rumors or justification for their judgment of me. Over the last 15 years or so, I've heard and seen all that. That's what so often makes me sad about the church and Christians. We work so hard to build people up and bring them to redemption only to relish in their demise when they fall.

I've stated it several times in this book—I am far from perfect. There are many, many choices I've made that I'm not proud of. All of them, along with every other heartbreaking moment and decision, nearly cost me my life. I had to finally make the decision that enough was enough. Yes, of course I have a past. Who doesn't? Sure, I own my past, but I chose a long time ago not to live there anymore. I read a quote recently by Christine Caine that drove this thought home for me. "Trying to hurt me by bringing up my past is like trying to rob my old house. I don't live there anymore. That ain't my stuff."

Recently, I traveled to Canada to sing in a few churches. If you've never been to Canada, I don't think I'm speaking out of line to say that Canadians aren't the most expressive lot in the free world. At concerts, they tend to sit still and just stare at you. I may try to crack a joke when speaking to the audience, and they give a confident but somber chuckle, maybe a gentle golf clap. What you don't see is outright hilarity or rolling in the aisles. There's no abundance of emotion or expression, at least not at a Christian concert. (I'm sure they're out of control for Michael Bublé.)

On this recent visit, I shared my story at all four locations. When our group was finished, I worried that I hadn't connected with the audience because there seemed to be an empty response during the concert.

I was shocked when many came up to me afterward in tears and told me, "You know when you said you were waist-deep? I'm in over my head, and I can't breathe. I don't know what to do." I looked them in the eye, took their hands, and asked, "Do you have a spouse? Do you have kids?" In each case, they nodded. I said, "You owe it to them to fight through this. But even more than for them, you owe it to yourself to not cut short the plan God has for you. If I had taken my own life, I would have missed out on miracles and opportunities—the vast and unbelievable plan that God had for my life." My prayer is that a time will come when these desperate people will hear this message of hope from their church.

Depression and anxiety are forms of mental illness. They aren't things that have manifested because of a great lack of faith in God; they are a sickness. It was very obvious that I was struggling—still struggle sometimes—with depression. It is real and far more prevalent than people care to admit. It can cripple a person. It can convince us that we have to only show the world our best, even when we don't have the energy anymore to keep the mask in place. So many people are fighting silently and losing against this disease. The church is a place where people should receive support, comfort, and help, but instead, most people refuse to acknowledge depression as anything other than a lack of faith or gratefulness.

When the church culture is a facade of perfection, we miss the whole point of why God created the church. Christ came for sinners. He created the family of God, the church, not to be a building but to be the people. It isn't the veneer; it's the beating hearts that matter. If we don't come together and stay together as a people and build one another up, bear one another's wounds, accept one another for who we are, which is flawed, imperfect, and sometimes ugly and miserable, then how are we going to get out there and tell the world about Christ? Why would anyone believe us or even care what we have to say when we can't even love our own? We *must* take care of each other first.

Since I was a child, I've watched the church kick their wounded, starting with my parents. What they went through at the hands of Christian people who claimed to be their friends unfortunately shaped the way I viewed relationships in the church. When people come forward to admit they made a mistake, they are told they're unfit to be a minister and are forced to step down. When I hear about church leaders or pastors pushing people out because they publicly confess sin or struggle, I want to look at them and ask, "Sir, with all due respect, can I check your browsing history from last week?"

Romans 3:10 (KJV) says, "There is none righteous, no, not one." If you've been around a church for any amount of time, you've heard this Scripture, and yet so many still try to act to the contrary like they are worthy and righteous and in a position to pass judgment on those who stray. Passing judgment on those who stray is actually straying itself. The real tragedy comes when you're on the receiving end of that judgment and unfair ridicule and mentally unprepared to handle it.

I had a friend who was a well-known speaker in full-time ministry at a large church. He was married with two children and battled depression. He reached out for help privately because he didn't want to portray weakness to his congregation. When you're the leader of a large congregation, people have expectations of you. The pedestal is tall and impervious, and your congregation will fall apart if you fall off or climb down that pedestal and admit you are broken. The pressure of bearing that weight can be crushing. People expect their pastors to be set apart because they are our leaders, but that is extremely unrealistic. Unfortunately, there are some pastors who act as if they're above reproach, and they tend to cast their human expectations onto their staff and their congregation.

This friend of mine was overwhelmed with the issues in his life, and he decided to confide in a trusted counselor to get some help. Unfortunately, the counselor betrayed his trust, broke the confidentiality agreement, and shared in casual conversation this pastor's struggles. The leadership at my friend's church confronted him about his depression and subsequent counseling, and as a result, he was asked to step down from his leadership position. Two days later, he took his own life.

Repentance is for everyone as long as there is true remorse, even those who do ghastly things that result in someone taking their own life. I believe part of that remorse must include owning up to the part they played. As I've said so many times in this book, I've been the recipient of amazing grace when I've made heinous mistakes, and that is something that only Jesus in His mercy can offer.

In my darkest days, my friend's story came so close to being my own. I felt I had nowhere to turn because if I shared the cycle of events that led to my crippling depression, almost death, then I, too, would be seen as unfit to serve the Lord again. It wasn't a risk I felt I could take. However, there is nothing wrong with admitting you have a chemical imbalance and need medication to correct the problem. I believe that God in all His might and wisdom gives people the brains to invent medication to help us. Who's to say that when you pray for healing God doesn't provide your healing in the form of a prescription? If you have heart disease, you take a pill. I took a low dose of antidepressants for about six to eight months, and if I hadn't had that, my brain would have never started firing correctly again. Do not be ashamed; step forward. Get the help you need. It's available to you.

I think about the story of the prodigal son. I'm amazed at that father and the love he had for both his sons. He loved the son who was dutiful, stayed home, did all the work, was responsible, and didn't spoil his birthright. He loved him the same as the younger son who said, "Dad, I don't want to be here anymore. Give me what's owed to me because I'm leaving." I was that younger son; this was my story. I took everything that was offered to me—my calling, my God-given gifts, even the people I traveled with. I took it all and ran with it. I squandered it because I was more worried about fulfilling my purpose and my desires than fulfilling the Father's desires for my life.

My dad often said to me, "The Bible says to humble yourselves before the Lord because if you don't, God will do it for you— and when He does it, it always hurts." I have no doubt that the Lord has humbled me, and my dad was right—it hurts. But the great thing about the prodigal son story is that in my moment of weakness and deepest desperation when I had reached the end of my strength, when my face was buried deep in the same slop the pigs ate, I was able to raise my face from that squalor and look up to heaven. I was ready to leave the life I'd chosen and go home and see my dad. I didn't know if my heavenly Father would welcome me. I couldn't offer Him perfect, but maybe He could at least let me work for Him.

You all know the end of the story. The prodigal son's dad didn't just give him a job; he gave him his finest robe, put a ring on his finger, and killed the fatted calf. He told all the servants to prepare a feast to celebrate because his son, who was lost, had come home.

This is a lesson I've learned about the God we serve. We can never fall so far that we reach the bottom of His love for us. I want so much for people to understand that no matter how far you go from home, God is always waiting, standing at the window, looking out at the horizon to catch sight of your return.

I'm okay admitting now that I'm not perfect. I don't wake up every morning to a rainbow outside my window and doves flying out my rear end. But I do wake up with a renewed perspective on life. I wake up knowing that God's not asking for perfection from me; He's asking for a purpose. He wants me to wake up each morning and say, "God, this is what I have to offer today. It's about 75 percent less than yesterday, but it's all Yours. Take it, and use it." And the wonderful thing about Jesus is that He takes what little we have and makes it enough.

I'm ending this book with a call for honesty. It's time for us as Christians to start telling the truth about life—the good and the bad. When I was growing up, I heard some old folks say, "The ground is level at the foot of the cross." I never understood what that meant until I was desperate for some level ground. Now I get it. We're all in need of forgiveness. From the top pastor in the highest-ranking church with the largest attendance in the country to the janitor who cleans the toilets, we are all the same. We are only as good as the grace we stand on.

When Jesus died on the cross, He died for each of us because He knew that in the end, we would all be desperate for His grace. I'm grateful that He gives second chances. I want to be the kind of man who gives second chances—someone who listens and presses in when things get messy and never the one who runs or pushes away when things aren't status quo. I can't say I won't make more mistakes, but I will do my best until my last breath to be a good steward of the opportunities and experiences God gives me.

As I sit here trying to figure out how to wrap this all up, I can't stop thinking about my friend Jarrid Wilson. He was a fierce advocate for mental health awareness, and he worked tirelessly to shed light on the terrible and very real toll it is taking and has taken on so many pastors, leaders, and church members. Even though we only spoke a few times, he had the uncanny ability to make me feel like I was being heard and that I was not alone in my struggle.

Sadly, he was also a prime example of someone who appeared to have it all together, but his struggle reached its end, and he succumbed to the darkness he had fought against for most of his life. Shortly after he passed away, I came across something he tweeted. "Loving Jesus doesn't always cure suicidal thoughts. Loving Jesus doesn't always cure depression. Loving Jesus doesn't always cure PTSD. Loving Jesus doesn't always cure anxiety. But that doesn't mean Jesus doesn't offer us companionship and comfort. He *always* does that."

Here's the message in all this: *you are not alone.*

I understand that sometimes you feel like you *are* alone, but you're really not. Ever. Regardless of how hard you try to push everyone away, Jesus never leaves. He sits and waits and moves when necessary, but He never leaves. Our enemy, Satan, the idiot of all idiots, will lie to you and tell you you're not enough . . . that you're not worth it . . . that no one will ever understand you . . . that the world would be better off without you. He didn't get the moniker the Father of Lies because he was such a nice guy. He is, in fact, a liar. I want you to know—God wants you to know—that as long as you have breath left in your lungs, you have purpose, and there is so much more value in you than you can see.

Never underestimate God's plan or how much He loves you. Regardless of who you are and what you've done, He loves you. He stands at the window looking out over the horizon, waiting for you to come back to him. He has no concern for what you've squandered. You're worth far more than any of that. He has no malice for the poor choices you've made. He bled for all of that long ago. "But God shows His love for us in that while we were still sinners, Christ died for us" (Rom. 5:8 ESV). If that isn't proof of how much He loves you, I don't know what else is.

"Greater love hath no man than this, that a man lay down his life for his friends" (John 15:13 KJV). Jesus not only loves you, but He is absolutely crazy about you and longs for you to know that you can trust Him. Rest assured that the Creator of your heart can repair it when it's broken.

I hope beyond hope that you will allow these words—my story—to sink into your soul, that it will help you know that you can and will overcome the battles you're facing and rest knowing there is purpose in both your past and in what lies ahead. You are beautifully and perfectly made and never alone or forgotten. So hold on, trust God, and for heaven's sake, please . . .

Keep breathing.

DISCOGRAPHY

TRUTH

More Than You'll Ever Imagine—1991
Praise—1991
Something to Hold On To—1992
TRUTH Sings the Word—1995
One—1996

AVALON

Avalon—1996
A Maze of Grace—1997
In a Different Light—1999
Joy: A Christmas Collection—2000
Oxygen—2001
O2 Avalon Remixed—2002
Testify to Love, Best of Avalon—2003
The Creed—2004
Stand—2006
Faith, a Hymns Collection—2006
*Another Time, Another Place, Timeless Christian
    Classics*—2008
Avalon, the Greatest Hits—2009
Called—2020

CANA'S VOICE

This Changes Everything—2016
Live at Champion Forest—2017
You Don't Wanna Miss This—2019

JODY MCBRAYER

This Is Who I Am—2002
Keep Breathing—2016
Christmastime—2017

"Someone Like You" (single) – with VOCTAVE—2016
"So Far, So Good" (single) – 2021

ACKNOWLEDGMENTS

There is absolutely no question in my heart or mind that if it weren't for Jesus Christ and His abundant and continual grace, I would not be here. While I can write and sing eloquent words of thankfulness and praise to Him, nothing will ever adequately describe how grateful I am. So I will just simply say, Jesus, thank You. I love You so much.

To Stephanie, I love you so very much. Next to Jesus, you occupy a place in my heart that no one else does or ever will. You and me forever.

To Sarah-Clayton, nothing makes me prouder than being your father. You are the gift that I do not deserve but that God gave me anyway. Never ever question how much you are loved.

To my mother, Yolie McBrayer, thank you for always being there for me and being a consistent source of encouragement and love throughout my entire life. I'm so thankful to God that I had parents like you and Pop. I love you, Ma.

To Natalie Hanemann for helping me walk out this journey. Your encouragement to tell my story has inspired me. Thank you for making the process so much easier.

To Casey Cease for believing in me way back when this whole idea started. I believe the reason I didn't write this book back then was because God had a few more details He wanted to include. Thank you for your patience and persistence.

To everyone at Lucid Publishing, thank you for believing in me and my story enough to put it out there. Also, thanks for your patience. Sorry I am so slow.

To Roger Breland, the times I spent with you and TRUTH were some of the most significant moments of my life. Thank you for always believing in me and never giving up on me. I love you, my friend.

To the strong men and women who have mentored, encouraged, and held me up during this process and throughout my life: Tim Johnson, James Lowe, Steve Berger, Chris Beatty, Marilyn Meberg, William Hinn, Lee Dunlap, James Neal, Matthew Cork, Gerald and Debbie Barnes, Janet and Doug Chandler, David and Kathryn Mier, Dr. Blake Lindstrom, Dr. Lynn Morrell, and Dr. William Anderson. I am here because you have spoken into my life in a significant way. I will be forever grateful to you all.